Editors

Kim Fields

Heather Douglas

Illustrators

Kevin McCarthy

Clint McKnight

Cover Artist

Brenda DiAntonis

Editor In Chief

Karen J. Goldfluss, M.S. Ed.

Art Production Manager

Kevin Barnes

Art Coordinator

Renée Christine Yates

Imaging

Rosa C. See

Publisher

Mary D. Smith, M.S.Ed.

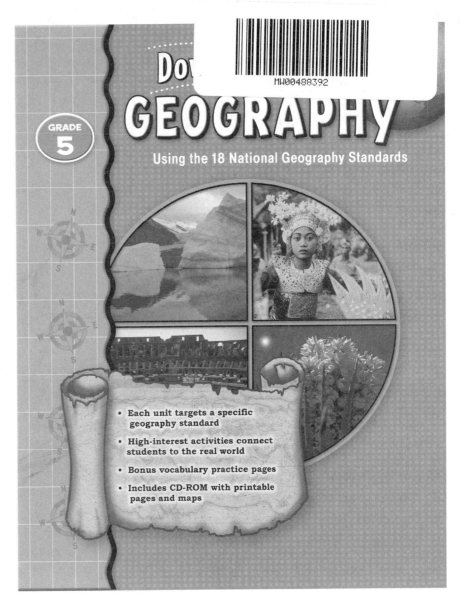

GRADE 5

GEOGRAPHY

Using the 18 National Geography Standards

- Each unit targets a specific geography standard
- High-interest activities connect students to the real world
- Bonus vocabulary practice pages
- Includes CD-ROM with printable pages and maps

MW00488392

Author

Ruth Foster, M.Ed.

Teacher Created Resources, Inc.

6421 Industry Way

Westminster, CA 92683

www.teachercreated.com

ISBN: 978-1-4206-9275-4

© 2008 Teacher Created Resources, Inc.

Made in U.S.A.

Teacher Created Resources

Table of Contents

Introduction

Geography Today

It has been said that our world is becoming smaller, largely due to advanced communication, economic partnerships, and worldwide trade markets. To understand, and eventually compete in, today's world, students must know more than physical characteristics of land and country borders. They must understand how communities and people interact, in part due to the geography of where they live. Students must understand that human actions can modify the physical environment and that changes occur in the use and importance of resources.

The goal of *Down to Earth Geography: Grade 5* is to help students become more geographically literate and better prepared for the global community. A variety of activities and high-interest readings take students on a journey that brings the world to them. At the end of the journey, students will have been introduced to the world of geography. In addition, they will have developed skills in assessing and understanding the world in spatial terms, places and regions, physical systems, human systems, environment and society, and the uses of geography.

About This Book

The units in this book are based on the National Geography Standards, which were developed by the Geography Education Standards Project and sponsored by the National Council of Geographic Education, the National Geography Society, the American Geographical Society, and the Association of American Geographers. These standards can be found in the book, *Geography for Life: National Geography Standards, 1994.*

Down to Earth Geography: Grade 5 is divided into 18 units. Each unit focuses on one of the 18 National Geography Standards listed on pages 6–7.

How to Use This Book

Information Pages

Each unit begins with an introductory page that explains basic information about the unit. The information on this page is written on a level that allows students to read about the topics addressed in the unit. It provides them with both useful and interesting information to whet their appetites for future learning.

The information page also introduces the vocabulary words that are used in each unit. Vocabulary words are bolded when they are first introduced in an activity. It is recommended that vocabulary words be discussed and defined when they appear in an activity, rather than out of context. (A reproducible Geography Word Log is provided on page 165 to be used for recording the vocabulary words and meanings as they appear in context. Students can write the words and meanings on the log. Reproduce copies as needed.) Vocabulary Practice activities for each unit can be found on pages 156–163.

The What I Do section on the information page gives students brief directions for the unit activities and summarizes the new knowledge they will gain after completing the unit.

Activity Pages

The activities in each unit vary in form and are written to inspire students to think about and respond to the content. Some activities require students to mark areas on maps. Others require answering multiple choice, true/false, or fill-in questions. Several exercises ask students to write sentences or list reasons to support their choices.

Although the activities are written at a level that allows students to complete them independently, it is recommended that teachers use a combination of independent, small group, and whole-class learning approaches for each unit. Sharing information, ideas, and responses to the activities will reinforce the students' understanding of each standard.

An Answer Key for the Activity Pages is provided on pages 151–155.

How to Use This Book (cont.)

Reproducible Pages

Reproducible Pages are included at the end of this book (see pages 166–176). This section includes two world maps, a map of each continent, and two versions of a U.S. map. Copy and distribute these pages for student reference (e.g., for an activity that includes locating a specific country in Africa, page 168 would be an excellent resource).

CD-ROM

Each CD-Rom includes all student pages and each reference map at the end of the book.

The student pages have been prepared as PDF files and can be printed from the CD. Print a master copy and reproduce as many as needed on a copier, or print as many copies as you wish right from the CD files. Pages are listed by the page numbers in the book and by the standards to which they are correlated. For example, **P_009 Standard 1** indicates that the content is from page 9, which appears in the standard 1 unit.

For printers capable of printing on transparency sheets, you can select specific student pages and maps to display on an overhead projector for whole-class viewing, discussion, or review.

The National Geography Standards

There are 18 National Geography Standards. All 18 standards are covered in this book. Each standard is covered in its own unit. Each unit has a series of Activity exercises. The Activity exercises were designed to meet student expectations as listed by the National Geography Standards. Listed below and on page 7 are the standards taught and reinforced in this book.

The World in Spatial Terms

Standard 1: How to use maps and other geographic representations, tools, and technologies to acquire, process, and report information

Standard 2: How to use mental maps to organize information about people, places, and environments

Standard 3: How to analyze the spatial organization of people, places, and environments

Places and Regions

Standard 4: The physical and human characteristics of a place

Standard 5: That people create regions to interpret Earth's complexity

Standard 6: How culture and experience influence people's perception of places and regions

Physical Systems

Standard 7: The physical processes that shape the patterns of Earth's surface

Standard 8: The characteristics and spatial distribution of ecosystems on Earth's surface

The National Geography Standards *(cont.)*

Standards 9–18

Human Systems

Standard 9: The characteristics, distribution, and migration of human populations on Earth's surface

Standard 10: The characteristics, distributions, and complexity of Earth's cultural mosaics

Standard 11: The patterns and networks of economic interdependence on Earth's surface

Standard 12: The process, patterns, and functions of human settlement

Standard 13: How forces of cooperation and conflict among people influence the division and control of Earth's surface

Environment and Society

Standard 14: How human actions modify the physical environment

Standard 15: How physical systems affect human systems

Standard 16: The changes that occur in the meaning, use, distribution, and importance of resources

The Uses of Geography

Standard 17: How to apply geography to interpret the past

Standard 18: To apply geography to interpret the present and plan for the future

Maps, Globes, and Finding Our Way Around

What I Need to Know

Vocabulary

- title
- legend
- key
- symbol
- cardinal directions
- intermediate directions
- vertical
- horizontal
- grid
- cartography
- cartographer
- equator
- Northern Hemisphere
- Southern Hemisphere
- lines of latitude
- parallels
- lines of longitude
- meridian
- prime meridian
- Eastern Hemisphere
- Western Hemisphere

What I Do

About Maps

A map is a valuable tool. We use maps to help us get where we want to go. We also use maps to show us different kinds of information. Today, most maps have certain elements in common. We use a system of lines to divide Earth into parts. We use compass points for directions. The lines and compass points help us locate where places are.

Complete the Activities. When you are done, you will know about the oldest known map in the world. You will know about a spy who risked death, all for a map. You will know what the lines on maps mean and how they help us divide Earth into parts.

Name _____ **Date** _____

Activity 1

The oldest known map in the world was drawn on a clay tablet. It was made in about 600 BCE and came from Babylon, a city that was located in present-day Iraq. The map shows Earth as a circle. Babylon is at the center of the circle, and the Tigris and Euphrates Rivers are on the map as well. Seven triangles are drawn on the edge of the circle, which is where strange beasts were supposed to live. Around the world was a vast ocean called the Bitter River.

Why was the oldest map drawn on a tablet of clay?

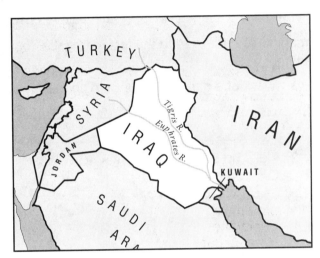

   A. The Babylonians liked big, heavy maps.

   B. Strange beasts lived all over Earth.

   C. Paper and printing were not yet invented.

   D. The soil around the Tigris and Euphrates Rivers is mostly sand.

On another sheet of paper, make a sketch of what the oldest known map looks like.

On the map on this page, find Iraq and the Tigris and Euphrates Rivers.

Activity 2

Maps were important because they showed trade routes. In the 15th and 16th centuries CE, the rulers of Spain and Portugal did not want other people to see their maps. They did not want people to know about their new Eastern trade routes.

In 1502, an Italian spy went to Lisbon, a city in Portugal. The spy posed as a horse dealer and smuggled a map out of Portugal. If he had been caught, he would have been killed.

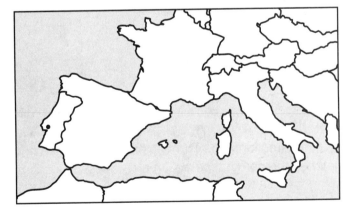

Why would the spy have been killed if caught?

   A. He was from Italy.

   B. He was a horse dealer.

   C. He pretended to be someone else.

   D. He had a map that showed new Eastern trade routes.

List three ways a map can be used today.

   1. _____

   2. _____

   3. _____

On the map, find and label the city of Lisbon and the countries of Spain, Portugal, and Italy.

Name _____   **Date** _____

Activity 3

The earliest known printed map was made in China in about 1155 CE. The map shows the Great Wall, which is about 1,500 miles (2,414 km) long and 25 feet (7.6 m) high. The Great Wall was built in order to keep out invaders.

Today, maps have basic elements, such as a title and a legend, or key. The **title** is a name given to the map to tell us what the map is of. A **legend**, or **key**, tells us what the symbols on a map mean. **Symbols** are shapes, lines, or little pictures used on a map.

Imagine you are making the first map to be printed.

1. Think of a name for your map and title it.

   _____

   _____

2. Make up symbols for the key and place them on the map.

> Key

Activity 4

The first magnetic compass was invented in China in the 11th century CE. It was made from a needle of iron that was put in a bowl of water. As it floated, it pointed roughly north-south along Earth's magnetic line.

From the story, you can tell that

   A. iron is only found in China.

   B. Earth has a magnetic line.

   C. needles were invented in the 11th century CE.

We use points on a compass as directions. The **cardinal directions** are north (N), east (E), south (S), and west (W). People use the saying, "Never Eat Soggy Worms" to help them remember how the directions go. The beginning letter of each word matches the cardinal points on a compass.

Never = _____   Eat = _____

Soggy = _____   Worms = _____

Fill in the cardinal directions on the map compass.

Find China on the map.

Is Iraq west or east of China? _____

Are Spain, Portugal, and Italy east or west of China?

_____

Name _____ **Date** _____

Activity 5

Sometimes cardinal directions are not enough, especially when we want to be more exact. When we want to be more exact, we use intermediate directions. **Intermediate directions** are points on the compass between the cardinal points.

One point is NE, and it falls between north and east. Another point is NW, and it falls between north and west. A third point is SE, and it falls between south and east. A fourth point is SW, and it falls between south and west.

Fill in the cardinal and intermediate points on the compass.

Complete each sentence with an intermediate direction.

Idaho is _____ of California.

California is _____ of Idaho.

Arkansas is _____ of Kansas.

Kansas is _____ of Arkansas.

New York is _____ New Mexico.

New Mexico is _____ of New York.

Use your own state to make up a question like the ones above. Your answer should be an intermediate direction. _____

_____

Activity 6

Maps have lines that are vertical or horizontal. **Vertical** lines go up and down, and **horizontal** lines go from side to side (like the horizon). The vertical and horizontal lines make a **grid**, which helps us pinpoint places more easily.

The library is located in the A2 grid.

Where on the grid are the following:

city hall?   _____

school?   _____

hospital?   _____

park?   _____

police station? _____

fire station?   _____

Name _____ **Date** _____

Activity 7

Cartography is the making and study of maps. A **cartographer** is a person who makes maps. The Greeks were the first cartographers to use grids. They also made lines on the globe.

The Greeks made a line we call the equator. The **equator** is a horizontal line that divides Earth in two. Above the equator is the **Northern Hemisphere**. Below the equator is the **Southern Hemisphere**.

Answer the questions below using complete sentences.

What is cartography? _____

What line divides Earth into the Northern Hemisphere and Southern Hemisphere?

_____

On the map below, find and label the *equator, Northern Hemisphere*, and *Southern Hemisphere*.

Which hemisphere do you live in? _____

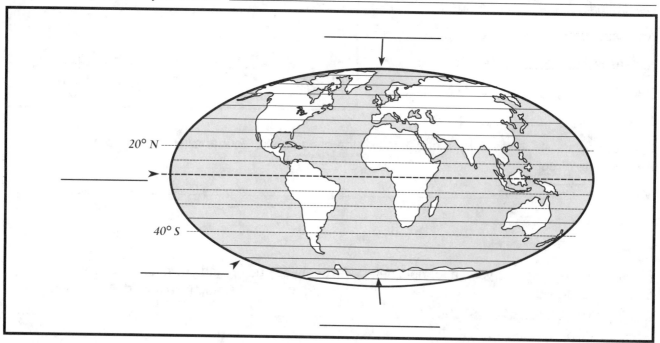

Activity 8

The equator is not the only horizontal line on the globe. **Lines of latitude**, also called **parallels**, are horizontal lines. Lines of latitude run parallel to each other, which means that they never touch. Lines of latitude are always the same distance apart.

The equator is at 0 degrees (0°). Latitude is measured from the equator. Latitude lines are measured from 0° to 90° from the equator to the South Pole, and from 0° to 90° from the equator to the North Pole.

On the map above, fill in the following words: *South Pole, North Pole, line of latitude.*

Number the latitude lines (0°, 10°, 20°, etc). Two of the lines have been marked for you.

Name _____ **Date** _____

Activity 9

To make a grid, one needs vertical and horizontal lines. Horizontal lines on a globe are called lines of _____ or _____ .

The vertical lines are called **lines of longitude**. Lines of longitude are also called **meridians**. The lines of longitude meet at the North Pole, the northernmost point on the globe, and at the South Pole, the southernmost point on the globe.

The _____ is a latitude line at 0°. What line of longitude is at 0°? The line of longitude at 0° is the **prime meridian**. The prime meridian was agreed upon in 1884, and it passes through Greenwich, England.

The prime meridian divides Earth in two. It does not divide it into north and south, but rather east and west. East of the prime meridian is the **Eastern Hemisphere**. West of the prime meridian is the **Western Hemisphere**.

On the map, fill in the following words: *prime meridian, equator, South Pole, North Pole, line of latitude, line of longitude, Western Hemisphere, Eastern Hemisphere.*

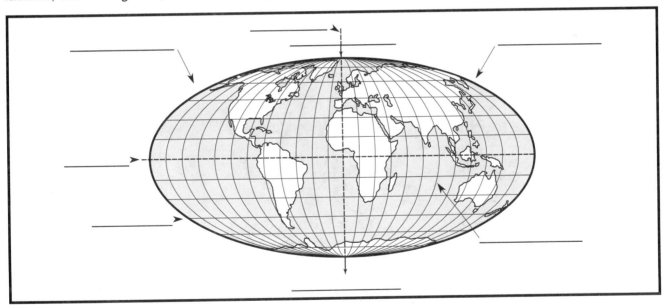

Activity 10

Read the story. On another sheet of paper, sketch a map that follows the path Mia and Jack took.

Mia and Jack were lost! They could hear a lion roaring to the **east** of them. Shaking with fear, they ran **north**. Suddenly Mia cried, "Oh, no! There is a tiger crouching in the grass! It is right in front of us!" The two children ran **west**. Jack said, "This can't be the way. Now we are in a desert. Look, there is camel! It is just to the **south** of us. Oh, how I want a drink!"

Mia and Jack would not give up. They turned **north**. When they stumbled upon some elephants, they slowly backed away, going **east**. They turned around when a gorilla started to beat its chest behind them. They ran **north** as fast as they could. They were about to cry when they heard a voice. The voice was stern. It said, "Listen! You two better not leave the group again! You know that the class should stay together when we take trips to the zoo!"

Name _____ **Date** _____

Activity 11

Longitude lines east of the prime meridian are numbered 1° to 179°. This is the Eastern Hemisphere. Longitude lines west of the prime meridian are numbered 1° to 179°. This is the Western Hemisphere. Halfway around Earth from the prime meridian is the 180° line.

On the map below, number the longitude lines 0°, 15°, 30°, 45°, 60°, 75°, and 90°. Two of the lines have been marked for you.

On the map, find Greenwich, England.

Name two countries in the Eastern Hemisphere. _____

Name two countries in the Western Hemisphere. _____

Do you live in the Eastern or Western Hemisphere? _____

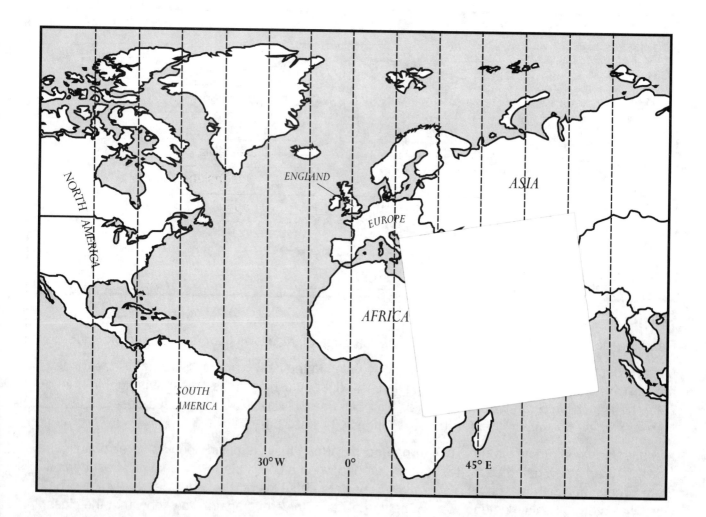

Name _____ **Date** _____

Activity 12

Use a world map or globe to answer the questions below.

Which country does this describe? 45° north latitude, 90° west longitude _____

Which hemispheres is the country in? (Pick two.) (Northern/Southern/Western/Eastern)

Which country does this describe? 30° south latitude, 120° east longitude _____

Which hemispheres is the country in? (Pick two.) (Northern/Southern/Western/Eastern)

Which country does this describe? 15° north latitude, 75° east longitude _____

Which hemispheres is the country in? (Pick two.) (Northern/Southern/Western/Eastern)

Which country does this describe? 15° south latitude, 45° west longitude _____

Which hemispheres is the country in? (Pick three!) (Northern/Southern/Western/Eastern)

Name the latitude and longitude for where you live. _____

Activity 13

Do you like roller coasters? Do you like being dropped? These roller coasters have the world's longest drops!

Roller Coaster	Drop	Location
Kingda Ka	418 ft (127 m)	New Jersey
Top Thrill Dragster	400 ft (122 m)	Ohio
Superman: The Escape	328 ft (100 m)	California
Tower of Terror	328 ft (100 m)	Queensland, Australia
Steel Dragon 2000	307 ft (94 m)	Japan

Looking at a bar graph helps you quickly compare the difference in drop heights of the roller coasters. Make a bar graph showing the drop heights.

In which two hemispheres is each roller coaster located?

Kingda Ka _____

Top Thrill Dragster _____

Superman: The Escape _____

Tower of Terror_____

Steel Dragon 2000 _____

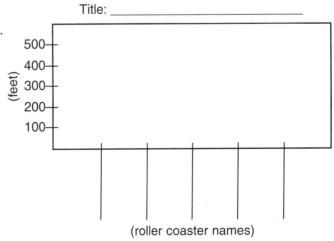

Title: _____

Mental Maps and Knowing Where We Are

What I Need to Know

About Mental Maps and Knowing Where We Are

You can find your way around your school. You do not use a paper map. You use a mental map, or a map in your head. We use mental maps to find our way around places we know. We also use mental maps to picture where we fit or are located in the world. Knowing continents and oceans helps us make a mental map of the world.

Vocabulary

- mental map
- peninsula
- continent
- isthmus
- ocean
- mountain
- mountain range

What I Do

Complete the Activities. When you are done, you will know about mental maps. You will know why the tallest mountain is not the tallest mountain! You will know about how much of Earth is covered in water and which of the oceans is the biggest. You will know in which ocean the most fish are caught.

Name _____ **Date** _____

Activity 1

Your teacher says, "Take this to the office." Because you know where to go, you do not get lost. You do not need a paper map to tell you how to get to the office. Instead, you use the map in your head, or a mental map. A **mental map** is an idea in your head of where something is and how to get to it.

Sketch a map of your school. Use the geographic images in your head to make the map.

On your map, show how to get to the cafeteria, library, office, and playground from your classroom.

In your key, tell what type of line goes where. Remember to title your map.

Title: _____

Activity 2

You should have a mental map of the United States. Answer the questions below using your mental map. Then, check your answers using a paper map of the United States. It is alright if you change your answers—but then change your mental map, too!

1. Is Utah farther west than North Carolina? _____

2. There are five Great Lakes. Does Wisconsin border a Great Lake? _____

3. Does Montana border an ocean or another country? _____

4. Is Tennessee near the West Coast? _____

5. Is Kansas to the east or west of Colorado? _____

6. Is Texas bigger than New Jersey? _____

7. A **peninsula** is a piece of land that juts into a body of water. It is surrounded by water on three sides. Is Ohio a peninsula? _____

8. Which state borders the Gulf of Mexico: Louisiana or Georgia? _____

9. Is Idaho farther east than Pennsylvania? _____

10. Which two states are not part of the U. S. mainland?

_____

Name _____ **Date** _____

Activity 3

There are seven continents in the world. A **continent** is a large land mass. You should have a mental map of the continents. Answer the questions below using only your mental map of the continents. Then check your answers using a globe or paper map. It is alright if you change your answers—but then change your mental map, too!

1. What is the only country that is an entire continent? _____

2. An **isthmus** is a narrow strip of land that connects two larger bodies of land. Which continent is connected to North America by an isthmus? _____

3. Which continent is south of Europe? _____

4. Which continent borders Europe to the east? _____

5. On which continent is the South Pole? _____

6. Which two continents are completely in the Northern Hemisphere?

   _____

7. Which continent's mainland is in the Northern Hemisphere but has islands in the Southern Hemisphere? _____

8. On which continent is the United States? _____

9. Which continent is the biggest? _____

10. Which continent is the smallest? _____

On another sheet of paper, sketch a map of the seven continents. Draw the equator on your map, too.

Activity 4

Sketch a map of where you live using your mental map. On the map, show things in your local community. Pick at least five places in addition to your house. Other places you might pick are your school, a friend's house, a store, a library, a park, a hospital, or a river. Use symbols to show where the places are in your community.

Remember to include a title and a key for your map. Put a compass on your map, too.

Title: _____

Key

Name _____ **Date** _____

Activity 5

Think of three places or cities that are in your state. Write a sentence describing each place.

1. _____

2. _____

3. _____

Sketch a map of your state. On your map, show the places you wrote about.

Give your map a title:

_____

Activity 6

Without looking, write who sits:

in front of you_____

behind you_____

next to you_____

Title: _____

Without looking, can you answer which states border your state? Who are your closest neighbors? Write which states border your state to the:

north _____

east _____

south _____

west_____

Check your answers on a paper map. Change them if you need to.

Sketch your state's outline. Place your neighboring states where they belong around its borders.

Name _____ **Date** _____

Activity 7

More than two-thirds of Earth is covered by water. Divide the bar below into three equal parts and color two of them. You colored in two-thirds of the bar.

From the bar, you can tell that Earth is mostly covered by:

A. land

B. water

An **ocean** is a large body of salt water that separates continents. There are four oceans. You should have a mental map of where the oceans are. The smallest ocean is on top of the world by the North Pole. It is the shallowest ocean and most of it is frozen all year. This is the . . .

A. Arctic Ocean

B. Indian Ocean

C. Pacific Ocean

D. Atlantic Ocean

Check your answer by looking at a map. Change it if you need to.

Answer the following questions using complete sentences.

What is an ocean? _____

How many oceans are there? _____

Activity 8

Your friend is outside your house and needs to get a clean pair of socks for you. Where are the socks in your room? You know because of your mental map. Draw a map for your friend. Draw a map from an outside door of your house to a clean pair of socks in your room.

Title: _____

Name _____ **Date** _____

Activity 9

The second-largest ocean has the most shipping because Europe and Africa are on one side, while North America and South America are on the other. Ships go back and forth between these continents carrying trade goods. This ocean is the least salty and where the most fish are caught.

What is the ocean? _____

One reason this ocean might be the least salty is because

   A. it has the most shipping   **C.** the most fish are caught in it

   B. it is the shallowest ocean   **D.** so many big rivers empty into it

One ocean lies almost entirely in the Southern Hemisphere. It is the third-largest ocean.

The _____ Ocean lies almost entirely south of the equator.

List the four oceans in order from smallest to largest.

   1. _____   **2** _____   **3.** _____   **4.** _____

Use your mental map to label the second and third largest oceans.

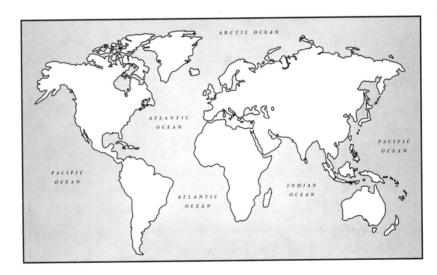

Activity 10

The biggest ocean covers more area than all the land on Earth! It is also the deepest ocean and has the lowest point on Earth, the Mariana Trench, which is 35,827 ft (10,920 m) below sea level.

Using your mental map of the four oceans, can you figure out which ocean this is? This ocean is to the west of the United States, between China and the United States. Many small volcanic islands lie in this ocean's waters.

The biggest ocean is the _____ Ocean.

It borders the _____ side of the United States.

Is the Arctic Ocean north or south of this ocean? _____

Check and change your answers if you need to.

Name _____ **Date** _____

Activity 11

A **mountain** is a part of the land that rises abruptly. It must be at least 1,000 feet (305 m) above the surrounding land. A **mountain range** is a group or chain of mountains.

On your mental map of the United States, you should have the following mountain ranges: Coastal Ranges, Sierra Nevada Mountains, Cascade Ranges, Rocky Mountains, Appalachian Mountains.

Write these mountain name ranges on the map below. Use the hints if you need to.

The Coastal Ranges are close to the Pacific Ocean.

The Sierra Nevada Mountains border California and Nevada.

The Cascade Ranges are in Oregon and Washington.

The Rocky Mountains are the largest mountain chain.

The Appalachian Mountains are farther east than the Rockies.

On the map, write the direction each mountain range is from where you live.

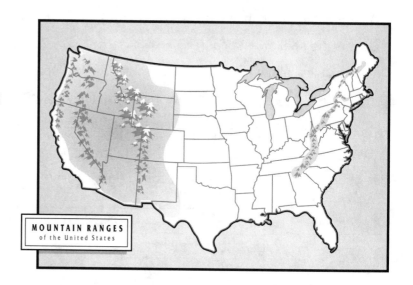

MOUNTAIN RANGES of the United States

Activity 12

Why is the tallest mountain in the world not actually the tallest mountain? The tallest mountain is in the Pacific Ocean. Since it is on the ocean floor, we can't actually see all of it. We only count the part we can see. Mauna Kea is a volcanic mountain that is part of Hawaii. It rises 33,476 ft (10,203 m) from the ocean floor. Only 13,798 feet (4,206 m) are above water.

Draw a picture of Mauna Kea. Think about where to draw your water line. Should it be drawn closer to the top or bottom of the mountain? Now, draw your water line.

Which ocean is Hawaii in?

_____

Which direction is Hawaii from where you live?

_____

Which, if any, mountain ranges separate you from Hawaii? _____

_____

Name _____ **Date** _____

Activity 13

The world's tallest mountain not covered by water is Mount Everest. Edmund Hillary and Tenzing Norway first climbed it in 1953. They used bottled oxygen in order to breathe. Why? Mount Everest is so high that the air at the top is very thin and there is not enough oxygen to survive for long periods of time.

Mount Everest is in China and Nepal. It is in the Himalayas, the mountain range which includes most of the world's tallest peaks.

On the map below, write the name and height of the highest mountain on each continent. Use your mental map of the continents to help you know which mountain is where.

Peak	Continent	Country(ies)	Elevation
Everest	Asia	China and Nepal	29,035 ft (8,850 m)
Aconcagua	South America	Argentina	22,834 ft (6,960 m)
Denali (McKinley)	North America	United States	20,320 ft (6,194 m)
Kilimanjaro	Africa	Tanzania	19,340 ft (5,895 m)
El'brus	Europe	Russia	18,510 ft (5,642 m)
Vinson Massif	Antarctica		16,067 ft (4,888 m)
Kosciuszko	Australia	Australia	7,310 ft (2,228 m)

The mountain range that includes most of the world's tallest peaks is called the _____.

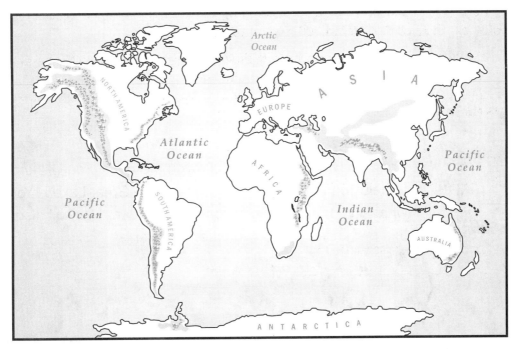

Directions and Where Things Are

About Directions and Where Things Are

Where do the clothes you are wearing come from? How about the food you eat? We use directions to answers these questions. Some directions are for things that are far away, and some directions are for things that are close together. When we map the world, we do more than write the names of places: we also think about how things are linked. We think about how far apart or close together things are. We draw maps so that we can tell by looking at them how far away or close something is in real life.

What I Need to Know

Vocabulary

- scale
- transported
- density

What I Do

Complete the Activities. When you are done, you will know a trick to help you remember the names of the Great Lakes. You will know what kind of music is considered American. You will also know how this music has ties to two other continents!

Name _____ **Date** _____

Activity 1

There are five Great Lakes. How can you remember them? Think of the word HOMES.

H stands for Huron

O stands for Ontario

M stands for Michigan

E stands for Erie

S stands for Superior

In each blank below, write the name of one of the Great Lakes using the map to help you.

The largest Great Lake is the largest freshwater lake in the world. This is Lake _____ .

The only one of the Great Lakes completely in the United States is Lake _____ . The United States and _____ have boundaries on the other four lakes.

One state that borders Lake Erie is _____ .

A city on Lake Michigan in Illinois is _____ .

Write the name of a lake to match each letter below:

H _____

O _____

M _____

E _____

S _____

Name _____ **Date** _____

Activity 2

A map is not a life-size representation of a place. The places and features on a map are reduced, or made smaller, than they are in real life. A map **scale** is used to show how close or far a place is compared to another place. For example, on some maps, one inch (2.5 cm) may mean one mile (1.6 km). An inch on the map is one mile in real life. On other maps, one inch may mean 100 miles (161 km). An inch on that map is 100 miles in real life.

Look at the map of the solar system. Look at the city map.

On which map does a distance of one inch (2.5 cm) indicate the:

biggest distance in real life? _____

smallest distance in real life? _____

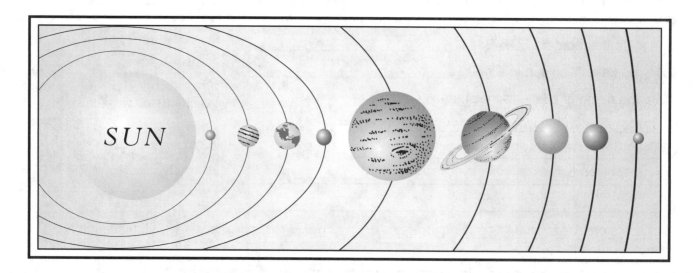

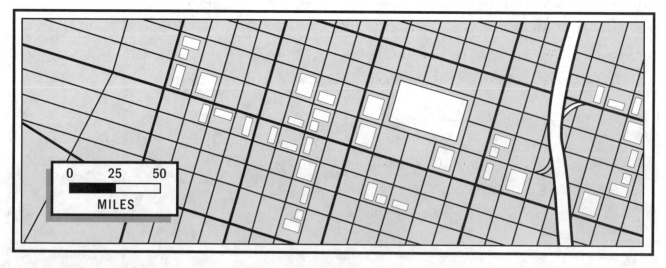

---

*Get ready for Activity 3. You will need a local map.

Name _____ **Date** _____

Activity 3

Use a local map for this activity.

1. Find and mark your school on the map.

2. Find and mark where you live on the map.

3. Find and mark where five of your classmates live.

4. Measure the distance from your home and your classmates' homes to the school.

Use the map scale to figure out the real-life distances.

Write the distances from question **4**: _____

Who lives the farthest? _____

Who lives the closest? _____

5. Draw a circle around the area your school serves.

Activity 4

Look at the subway map. This map is not drawn to scale. This means you cannot tell what the distance between the stops is. You can tell (pick two)

A. how fast the subway train is going

B. what stop is before and after each stop

C. at what stop you can catch different trains

Lindy gets on at station B. She is going to the zoo. To get to the zoo, she will get off at station N. Lindy will need to first

A. get on a 2 Train heading east toward H

B. get on a 2 Train heading west toward O

C. get on a 1 Train heading south toward A

D. get on a 1 Train heading north toward G

If Sarah goes to the zoo from station D, she will need to

A. get on a 2 Train heading east toward O

B. get on a 2 Train heading west toward H

C. get on a 1 Train heading south toward A

D. get on a 1 Train heading north toward G

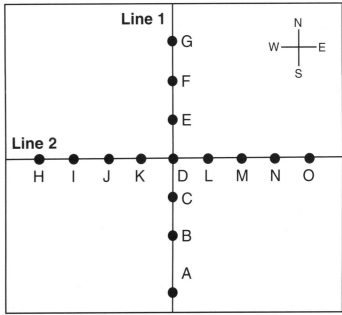

Name _____   **Date** _____

Activity 5

Alberto sat down to lunch in Arkansas. He had a tuna sandwich and some milk. The tuna came from Massachusetts, and the wheat for the bread was grown in Kansas. The milk was from a dairy in Missouri. He also had grapes that were grown in California, apple slices from Washington, and carrots that were grown in Rhode Island.

On the map, draw lines to show how the food for Alberto's lunch got to him.

Make a legend showing which line is for each food. Your lines might be solid, dotted, or dashes and dots.

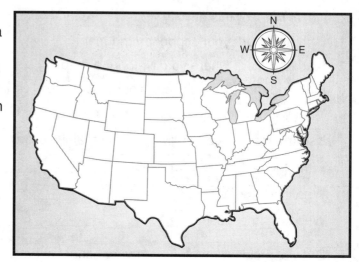

Activity 6

Mr. Echohawk told his students to look at the labels on their clothes and shoes:

- 7 items were made in the Philippines
- 16 items were made in Costa Rica
- 12 items were made in India
- 8 items were made in Bangladesh

- 8 items were made in the United States
- 15 items were made in China
- 9 items were made in Mexico
- 2 items were made in Haiti

Make a bar graph showing where the items were made and how many came from each place. Write a title for your bar graph.

Look at the labels on some of the clothes and shoes that students are wearing in your class. Where were the items made?

Title: _____

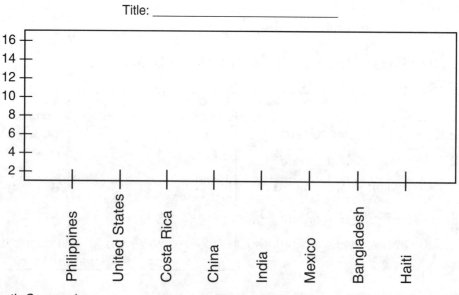

Name _____　　**Date** _____

Activity 7

Think again about the students and items in Mr. Echohawk's class. Draw lines on the map below from where the items were made to the United States. The items were made in the Philippines, Costa Rica, China, India, Mexico, Bangladesh, and Haiti.

Think about where the items were made. How do you think they were **transported**, or moved, to the United States?

_____

_____

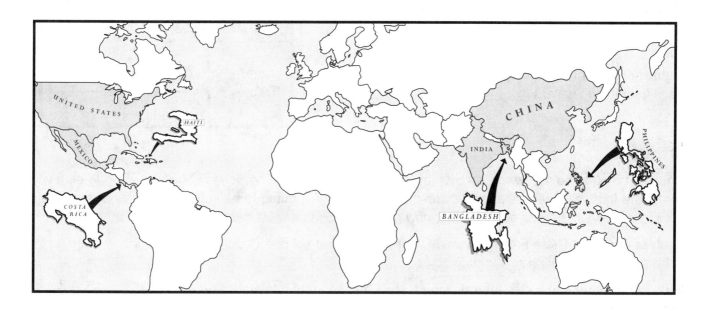

Do you think people in the United States used as many items made in other places long ago? Why or why not?

_____

_____

Why would items be made in other countries and sold in the United States?

_____

_____

Activity 8

What if a big storm hit where you live? What if high winds knocked over telephone and power lines and trees fell and blocked roads? What if roads and fields were flooded with water? What if no one could get to you and you could not get out for three days?

On a separate piece of paper, write a story about what it would be like for you during those three days. Use these words in your story: *fresh food, mail, school, friends, heat, information, clean, cooking.*

Name _____   **Date** _____

Activity 9

Density refers to how thick or crowded something is. When something is dense, its parts are close together.

Look at the map to the right. In which grid section would you expect there to be the:

highest density of people working in offices?

_____

highest density of people living in houses?

_____

highest density of mosquitoes? (Hint: mosquitoes lay eggs in standing water.) _____

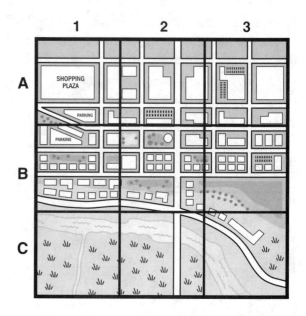

Activity 10

There is going to be a new restaurant that will serve drinks and sandwiches. There is going to be a new store that sells medical supplies and medicine. There is going to be a new school for elementary school students. There is going to be a new gas station. Where should each new place be located?

Look at the map. There are eight circles on the map. Choose one circle for the restaurant's, store's, school's, and gas station's location.

Tell why you chose to locate the restaurant, store, school, and gas station where you did.

restaurant: _____

store: _____

school: _____

gas station: _____

Name _____ **Date** _____

Activity 11

Jazz is a type of American music that started around 1890. Its melody and rhythms came from Africa. Africans who were brought to the United States as slaves used to sing work songs, spirituals, and many other types of songs that had African elements, or parts. When the melodies and rhythms were combined, jazz became a new form of music. It began in the South and spread north and west across the United States. Today, jazz is played all over the world.

Why might jazz have started in the South?

   A. Jazz is the only type of American music.

   B. Only people in the South knew how to sing.

   C. There were more slaves in the South than in other parts of the country.

   D. People in the North did not know how to combine rhythms and melodies.

On the map, draw arrows showing how jazz spread across the United States.

Try to do this with your mental map first! Then check and change your answers if you need to.

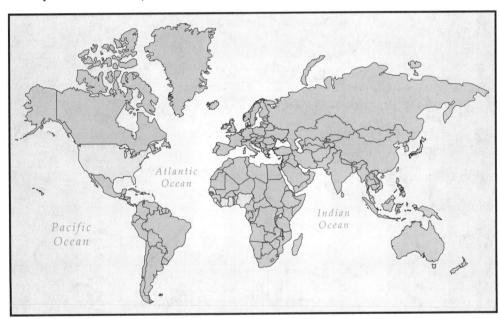

Activity 12

Jazz is a type of American music, but it has ties to Gambia, Ghana, Ivory Coast, Nigeria, Senegal, and Sierra Leone. Many of the slaves brought to North America came from these countries.

On the map, find and mark Gambia, Ghana, Ivory Coast, Nigeria, Senegal, and Sierra Leone.

Now, find Belgium on the map. (Hint: Belgium is not in Africa or North America!)

Jazz has ties to Belgium, too! Adolph Sax, who was born in Belgium in 1814, invented the saxophone. When he invented the saxophone, no one thought it was a serious instrument. Today, the saxophone is important to jazz music. Many jazz bands feature one or even two saxophones.

Why does jazz have ties to a country in Europe? _____

Name _____   **Date** _____

Activity 13

Look at the picture. Write five sentences about the picture. In each sentence, tell where an item is in relation to other items in the picture. Use directional words such as *north*, *east*, *south*, and *west*. Use positional words such as *closer than*, *next to*, and *beside*.

1. _____

2. _____

3. _____

4. _____

5. _____

Different Places, Different People

About Different Places and People

We can describe a place by its land, its plants and animals, and by its people. The land and the people together shape a place. For example, many people may go to one place because the soil is rich and fertile and they can grow crops. On the other hand, the people can turn the fertile soil into a desert where nothing can grow.

What I Need to Know

Vocabulary

- region
- reef
- gulf
- population
- satellite picture
- vegetation
- windward
- leeward

What I Do

Complete the Activities. When you are done, you will know the location of the wettest place in the United States. You will also know about a Ring of Fire, the location of the world's largest man-made reef, and the making of a man-made desert.

Name _____ **Date** _____

Activity 1

Indonesia is a country in Asia. It is made of over 17,500 islands. Bali is a small island east of Java, a bigger island. Both Bali and Java are part of Indonesia.

Orchestras are made up of instruments. In Bali, the traditional orchestra has almost all percussion instruments. It is made up of gongs, cymbals, and xylophones. Using all these instruments, you make a sound by hitting it. With percussion instruments, you strike something to make a sound.

Which of these is a percussion instrument?

A. drum   **C.** violin

B. saxophone   **D.** trumpet

Which instruments make up your local orchestra?

_____

On the map, find Indonesia, Bali, and Java.

Which direction are you from Bali? _____

Which two hemispheres is Bali in? _____

Activity 2

A **region** is a geographical area. All over the world there are different regions with different climates. Some are hot, some are cold, some are dry, and some are wet.

The wettest place in the United States is on the top of Mount Wai´ale´ale, which is in Hawaii on the island of Kauai. It rains an average of 335 days per year, with an average rainfall of 460 inches (12 m) each year! That's over 38 feet of rain!

On the map, find Hawaii and the island of Kauai. Describe Kauai's location in relation to the island of Hawaii. _____

Is Hawaii in the largest or second-largest ocean?

_____

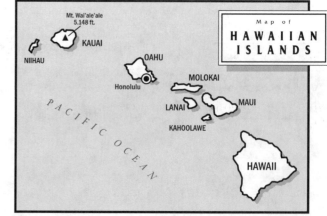

On the average, how many days a year *doesn't* it rain on Mount Wai´ale´ale?_____

How much rain falls in your region on average per year?_____

How many days does it rain in your region on average per year? _____

Name _____ **Date** _____

Activity 3

The map below is a climate and weather map. It shows the weather conditions across the United States for one day. Use the map to answer the questions.

Deserts are most likely located in

   A. New York   **B.** California

On the average,

   A. it gets warmer as you go north

   B. it gets warmer as you go south

True or false?

It only rains when it is cold. _____

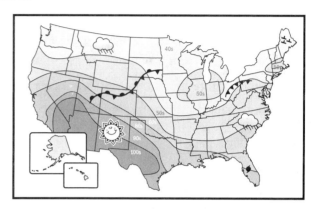

Look in your newspaper for a daily weather map.
Write the weather for your region. Did today's weather match the forecast on the map?

_____

Activity 4

You know North America and South America, but what is Central America? Central America is not a continent; it is a region of North America. Central America is made of the countries Belize, Costa Rica, El Salvador, Guatemala, Honduras, Nicaragua, and Panama.

Many people in this region speak Spanish. This may be because

   A. Spanish explorers and settlers started arriving in the early 1500s.

   B. no one spoke until Spanish explorers and settlers arrived in the early 1500s.

On the map, write the name of each Central American country.

Which continent is Central America a part of? _____

Which two countries in Central America do not border
both the Pacific Ocean and the Caribbean Sea?

_____

Within which two hemispheres is Central America
located?

_____

What is the main language spoken in your region?
Why?

_____

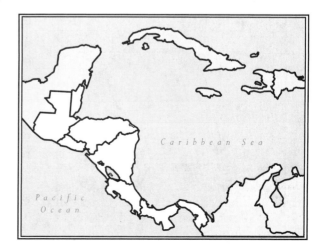

Name _____   **Date** _____

Activity 5

One region known as the Ring of Fire is a narrow belt around the Pacific Ocean. Most of Earth's active volcanoes are on this belt. There are over 500 active volcanoes, half of which are in the Ring of Fire.

Why are there so many volcanoes ringing the Pacific? Earth's crust is not one solid piece. It is made of huge plates that float on a thick layer of very hot, sometimes melted rock. In the Pacific, the plates are rubbing against one another, which causes earthquakes and volcanic eruptions.

Name two countries that lie in the Ring of Fire . . .

in the Southern and Western Hemisphere

_____

in the Southern and Eastern Hemispheres:

_____

in the Northern and Western Hemispheres:

_____

in the Northern and Eastern Hemispheres:

_____

Is Africa in the Ring of Fire?

_____

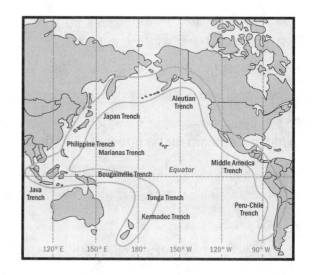

Activity 6

People can change the land by cutting down trees, planting new crops, building dams, and paving roads. People can also make **reefs**, which are ridges of sand, coral, or bedrock under water.

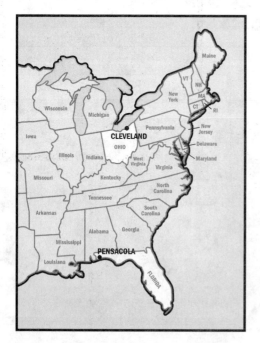

The world's largest man-made reef was created in 2006. It is 888 feet (271 m) long. It is in the Gulf of Mexico off the coast of Pensacola Beach, Florida. It was created when an old U.S. Navy ship was sunk. Florida expects money to be spent in their state because of the reef. How? Fish and other marine life will come to live on and around the man-made reef. Then fishermen and sports divers will come, too.

What might the fisherman and sports divers spend money on in Florida? _____

Find Pensacola, Florida. Which direction is it from where you live? _____

Name two states you would cross over if you flew from Pensacola to Cleveland, Ohio. _____

_____

On the map, label the Gulf of Mexico.

Name _____ **Date** _____

Activity 7

What is a gulf? A **gulf** is a large area of sea that is partly surrounded by land. Use the map below to answer the questions.

Which country is not part of the land that surrounds the Persian Gulf?

   A. Iraq

   B. Oman

   C. Saudi Arabia

   D. United Arab Emirates

Iran borders two gulfs. Name the gulfs.

   1. _____

   2. _____

What is the name of the gulf in East Africa?_____

Which gulfs are to the east and west of Mexico? _____

Use a complete sentence to answer this question: What is a gulf?_____

_____

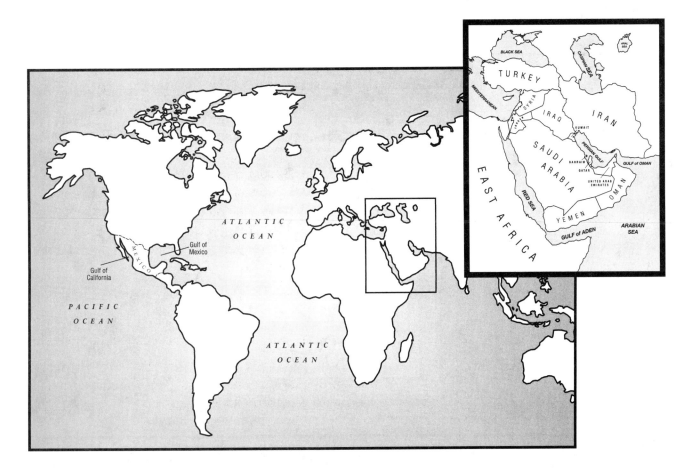

Name _____ **Date** _____

Activity 8

A **population** is the total number of people in one place. Some countries have higher populations than others, which means that they have more people living there. On the map below, find the following countries and write the number they were ranked in population in 2005.

1—China	6—Pakistan
2—India	7—Bangladesh
3—United States	8—Russia
4—Indonesia	9—Nigeria
5—Brazil	10—Japan

In 2005, one-fifth of the world's population lived in China. Color in one part of the bar to show 1/5.

Why might one country have a higher population than another? _____

Which of the countries listed above is in Africa? _____

Which of the countries listed above are closest to your own country? _____

Name _____ **Date** _____

Activity 9

Some countries are more densely populated than others. Imagine that every country is divided into squares that are all the same size. Big countries will have more squares than little countries. The population number is then divided into the number of squares a country has. The number we get gives us the density of a certain country. The number does not tell us exactly where people live in the country, but it does tell us how much land there is per person in the country.

1—Monaco	6—Bangladesh
2—Singapore	7—Bahrain
3—Vatican City	8—Taiwan
4—Malta	9—Barbados
5—Maldive	10—Nauru

On the map below, find and label the 10 most densely-populated countries (listed above). Write the number they were ranked in 2005.

Compare this map to the map in Activity 8.

Does a country have to be big in size to be densely populated?

_____

Is a city area or country area more likely to be densely populated?

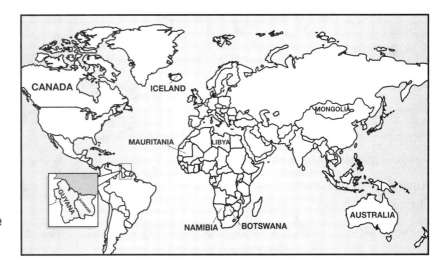

Activity 10

The countries listed here are not the most densely populated. They are the most sparsely populated, which means they have the lowest density per square mile or kilometer.

Find the countries on the map above. Write the number each was ranked in 2005. Use a different color marker than you did for Activity 9. Make a key for your map, that tells what the two colors are for.

It is likely that large areas of these countries are

   A. very dry or very cold

   B. good for growing crops

Which direction is Libya from Suriname?

_____

Rank/Country	Density per sq mile (sq km)
1—Mongolia	4.6 (1.8)
2—Namibia	6.4 (2.5)
3—Australia	6.8 (2.6)
4—Suriname	7.0 (2.7)
5—Botswana	7.3 (2.8)
6—Iceland	7.7 (3.0)
7—Mauritania	7.8 (3.0)
8—Libya	8.5 (3.3)
9—Canada	9.3 (3.6)
10—Guyana	10.1 (3.9)

Name _____ **Date** _____

Activity 11

There is a man-made desert in Kalmykia, which is a republic in southern Russia on the continent of Europe. It is on the northwest shore of the Caspian Sea. Kalmykia's soil was rich and black, perfect for raising sheep and other animals. In the 1950s, more than a million sheep were brought to Kalmykia. The sheep were a special kind with soft wool, but they also had very sharp hooves!

The sheep ate all the grass, and their sharp hooves cut through the soil like razors. The land was ruined. **Satellite pictures** are pictures taken from space. In satellite pictures, Kalmykia now looks like the moon—a large, empty area.

From the story, you can tell that

   A. satellite pictures are not useful

   B. all animals have the same type of hooves

   C. too many animals in one area can be harmful

   D. animals were not raised in Kalmykia before the 1950s

Put an **X** on the map where Kalmykia is.

Russia is on two continents. The Ural Mountains are the dividing line.

On the map, find the Ural Mountains. Is Kalmykia east or west of the Urals?_____

Activity 12

People can look at satellite photos to see where vegetation grows. **Vegetation** is plant and tree growth. Often, one side of a high mountain range has lots of vegetation, while the other has very little. Why is this?

Warm, moist air flows up from coastal regions. The air hits the **windward** side of a mountain, which is the side that is in the direction that the wind blows. The air is pushed up and gets cool, and the cooled water vapor in the air forms clouds. Often, it falls as rain. The other side of the mountain is the **leeward** side, which is the side that is protected from the wind and rain. Therefore, little rain falls on the leeward side. Often, there are plains or deserts there because the windward side of the mountain blocks the moist air.

On another sheet of paper, draw a picture of a mountain.

Label the windward and leeward sides of your mountain.

On the proper side:

   • show an ocean

   • show clouds and rain

   • show vegetation

Name _____ **Date** _____

Activity 13

Think about where you live. List four things about the landforms and climate. Is your region made up of flat plains, mountains, or deserts? Are there rivers, lakes, or oceans nearby?

1. _____
2. _____
3. _____
4. _____

List four things about the community where you live. You might mention what types of jobs there are, what people do for fun, what languages people speak, etc.

1. _____
2. _____
3. _____
4. _____

How do the landforms and climate have an effect on where people live? _____

How do the landforms and climate have an effect on what people do? _____

Places with Things in Common

What I Need to Know

Vocabulary

- residential
- industrial
- commercial
- recreational
- carnivorous
- marsh
- biome
- Polar Region
- Arctic Circle
- Antarctic Circle
- Tropic of Cancer
- Tropic of Capricorn
- tropics
- temperate
- boreal
- deciduous
- coniferous
- evergreen
- tundra
- permafrost

About Places with Things in Common

The world can be divided into regions. The regions are in different places and on different continents. Still, the regions have things in common. The plants and animals may be similar. The regions may have the same climate and some of the same landforms. People in the region may speak the same language.

What I Do

Complete the Activities. When you are done, you will know about an animal with a built-in life preserver, a plant that eats frogs, and a place on Earth that scientists think is the most like Mars.

Name _____ **Date** _____

Activity 1

Imagine that you are a reporter interviewing a person who is 100 years old. You want to find out about when this person was young and how things have changed in your region since then. On the lines below, write four questions about the following: transportation, shopping, habits, work, or land.

 1. _____

 2. _____

 3. _____

 4. _____

Write what you think the person you are interviewing might say in answer to two of your questions.

 1. When I was little, _____

 2. When I was little, _____

Activity 2

We divide the world into regions. We have climate regions, language regions, and vegetation regions. We even have regions inside a city.

We can describe the regions within a city: A **residential** area is where people live. An **industrial** area is where there is a lot of industry, which means any branch of business or manufacturing. When you manufacture something, you are making goods. Machines are used to make a lot of goods. A **commercial** area is where things are sold. A **recreational** area is where people go to have fun.

Label each picture as either *residential, industrial, commercial*, or *recreational*. Use each word once.

supermarket

_____

retirement community

_____

baseball field

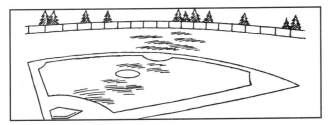

_____

computer-parts factory

_____

Name _____   **Date** _____

Activity 3

Can a plant eat a frog, a bird, or even a small rodent? (A rodent is a small animal with sharp teeth for gnawing. Rats, mice, squirrels, and rabbits are rodents.) The Nepenthes pitcher plant can!

The Nepenthes pitcher plant grows 30 to 40 inches (76–102 cm) tall. Part of the plant looks like a pitcher. The pitcher part is 12 inches (30 cm) tall, with slippery inner walls. The plant attracts prey into its pitcher with a sweet-smelling nectar and the water that collects in the bottom. When a frog or other creature slides down the slippery inner walls, the lid of the pitcher closes. It takes one to two weeks for the plant to digest its meal.

The Nepenthes pitcher plant lives in Southeast Asia.

Which country is not in Southeast Asia?

A. Laos

B. Japan

C. Cambodia

D. Malaysia

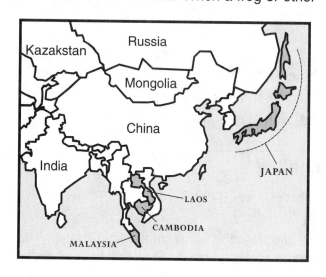

Activity 4

Plants that eat meat are **carnivorous**. There are about 600 different kinds of carnivorous plants. Most carnivorous plants live in **marshes**, which are areas of wet, low-lying land. A marsh can be fresh or salty, and it is usually near a river or seacoast. Marsh soil is usually low in nitrogen.

Like other plants, carnivorous plants make most of their energy from sunlight but to get enough nitrogen, they eat meat. Since the plants do not have teeth, they make special fluids that help them digest their prey.

How do carnivorous plants get most of their energy?

_____

What is marsh soil usually low in?

_____

True or False: Carnivorous plants have teeth.

_____

True of False: Marshes are always salty.

_____

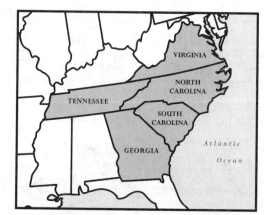

The Venus flytrap is a carnivorous plant that lives in North Carolina and South Carolina. Find these states on the map. Name the states to the north, south, and west of the Carolinas.

Name _____ **Date** _____

Activity 5

Sometimes the world is divided into regions by language. There are about 3,000 spoken languages in the world today. Listed below are the top 10 "first" languages. A first language is the language you learn to speak first. Many people speak more than one language. In fact, some countries have more than one official language.

1. Chinese (Mandarin)	**4.** Hindi	**7.** Russian	**9.** German
2. Spanish	**5.** Portuguese	**8.** Japanese	**10.** Chinese (Wu)
3. English	**6.** Bengali		

On the map below write the number of the language in at least one country where it is a "first" language.

Hint: Hindi is spoken in I __ __ __ __ . Bengali is spoken in B __ __ __ __ __ __ __ __ h.

What languages can students in your class speak? _____

_____

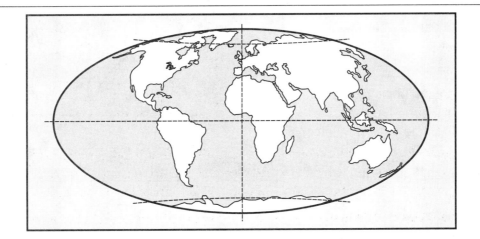

Activity 6

Earth can be divided into approximately 10 different natural regions called **biomes**. Each biome is a special mix of landforms, climate, animals, and plants. The coldest biomes are the **Polar Regions**.

The Polar Regions are around the North and South Poles. They are frozen deserts that are covered in ice all year long. The Polar Region near the North Pole and above the **Arctic Circle** is called the Arctic. It is a solid mass of frozen ocean. The Polar Region near the South Pole and below the **Antarctic Circle** is called the Antarctic. The Antarctic is much colder than the Arctic because it is a mass of frozen land.

Which is colder?

   A. the Arctic   **B.** the Antarctic

Why? Answer using a complete sentence. _____

_____

On the map above, find and label the North and South Poles. Find and label the Arctic Circle and the Antarctic Circle.

Name _____ **Date** _____

Activity 7

On the map below, you will see there are two lines that are imaginary, like the equator. Still, they help us divide Earth into regions. One line is the **Tropic of Cancer,** and the other line is the **Tropic of Capricorn**.

The Tropic of Cancer is in the _____ Hemisphere.

The Tropic of Capricorn is in the _____ Hemisphere.

They are lines of (latitude/longitude). _____

The **tropics** lie between the Tropic of Cancer and the Tropic of Capricorn. Tropical rain forests and tropical grasslands are two of the biomes found in this region.

Tropical regions are much warmer than Polar Regions because

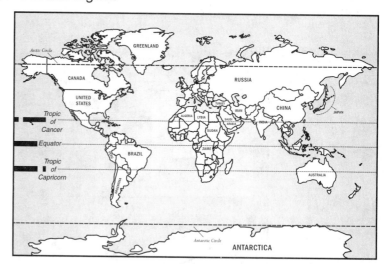

   A. tropical regions are closer to the equator

   B. tropical regions are farther away from the equator

Do you live in the tropics? _____

Do you live closer to the Tropic of Cancer, the Tropic of the Capricorn, the Arctic Circle, the Antarctic Circle, or the equator?

_____

Name one country on each continent that is in the tropics.

Activity 8

The regions between the Arctic and Antarctic Circles and the Tropics of Cancer and Capricorn are called **temperate** zones. Temperate forests and cool grasslands are two of the biomes found in these areas. Cool, or **boreal**, forests lie at the far end of the temperate zone in a few places. They extend just into the Polar Regions.

On the map, color in the polar, tropical, and temperate zones. Make a key showing which color stands for each zone.

Which zone do you live in? _____

Name one country on each continent that falls in a temperate zone. _____

_____

What is the only continent you cannot do this for? _____

Name _____ **Date** _____

Activity 9

Below, choose which animal—giraffe, walrus, or
skunk—matches the clues. Write which zone they
live in: temperate zone, Polar Region, or tropics.

This animal has a built-in life preserver. It has air pouches
around its neck. When it wants to float and sleep at sea, it
fills the pouches with air. The air and the animal's blubber are
enough to keep the animal afloat. Blubber is a layer
of fat which helps keep the animal warm.

animal— _____ zone— _____

This animal has a built-in secret weapon. It can produce a sticky, smelly liquid called musk. These
animals don't just squirt—they aim! They can hit targets 15 feet (5 m) away. As babies, these animals
can shoot musk before they can walk.

animal— _____ zone— _____

This animal is the tallest in the world. It has seven bones in its neck, just like you. The difference is
this animal's neck bones are much bigger. Each bone can be over 10 inches (25 cm) high!

animal— _____ zone— _____

Name another animal that lives in each zone: _____

Activity 10

Below, list which zone—polar, temperate, or tropical—being described.

Plants near the ground of this region have broad, flat leaves. The broad, flat leaves allow the plant
to absorb as much sunlight as possible. They need to absorb as much sunlight as they can because
the taller plants block out the sun. Leaves on plants near the ground often have waxy surfaces and
pointed tips, which allows water to run off easily.

zone— _____

Many forests in this zone are **deciduous**. Deciduous trees lose their leaves in the winter.

zone— _____

Only at the very edge of this zone do cool (boreal) forests grow. The forests are made of **coniferous
evergreens**. Evergreens do not lose their leaves. Coniferous trees are cone-bearing.

zone— _____

_____ trees lose their leaves in the winter.

_____ trees do not lose their leaves in winter.

_____ trees are cone-bearing.

Which country do you think has boreal forests?

A. Brazil　　　　　　　　**B.** Sweden

Name _____ **Date** _____

Activity 11

There is a place on Earth that scientists consider to be most like Mars. This is because it has dry valleys, and it has not rained there for over two million years. Falling snow evaporates before it hits the ground. The air is so dry that nothing decomposes or rots. In fact, there are dead seals scattered around the valleys. Some of the seals are over 1,000 years old! Where is this place?

This is a desert. It is not a hot desert, but a cold desert. It is in Antarctica. Only about two percent of Antarctica's land is exposed. The rest of the land is covered in ice. Scientists think the exposed, dry valleys may be like Mars.

When something is exposed, it is

A. covered   **B.** not covered

There are 100 squares in the box to the right. Only color two of them. That shows how much of Antarctica's land is not covered in ice.

The far north of Siberia in Russia is a cold desert. On the map below, find Russia. Put an **X** in the far north of Siberia.

Activity 12

Think about the region where you live. Think about its plants and animals, and its industrial, commercial, residential, and recreational areas. Also think about the languages spoken in your region. Now, compare your region to another continent in a different biome.

List six things that are the same or different about the regions.

1. _____

   _____

2. _____

   _____

3. _____

   _____

4. _____

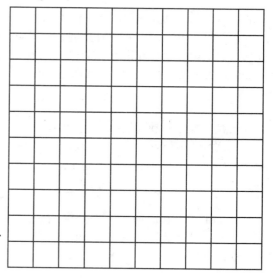

5. _____

6. _____

Name _____ **Date** _____

Activity 13

In a **tundra** biome, the top of the ground thaws during the short, warm season but underneath there is a layer of ground that never melts! It is called **permafrost**. Tundra biomes are found below the Polar Regions in the Arctic.

Low-growing shrubs and flowers bloom in the tundra in the growing season. Migrating animals, such as moose and caribou, leave their winter homes in the south. They come north to feast on the plants. These same animals will head south when winter starts.

Why are there no trees or forests in the tundra?

A. The moose and caribou eat all the leaves before they can grow.

B. The trees cannot put down deep roots into the hard ground to hold themselves up.

Tundra regions are (below/above) the Tropic of Cancer.

In which country can you find tundra?

A. Canada

B. Switzerland

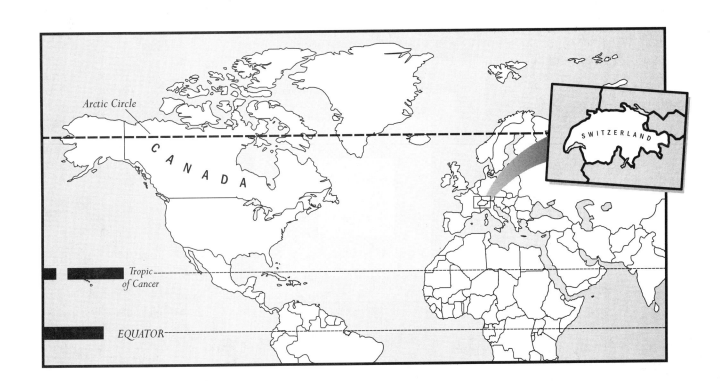

How We Think About Different Places and Where We Live

What I Need to Know

About How We Think About Different Places

Each of us has places we think are more important than others. A place that we think is important may not be important to someone else. Your perspective is your point of view, or how you look at something. Everyone does not have the same perspective. We look at things with different views. Sometimes listening to other people's perspectives can change our own.

Vocabulary

- perspective
- point of view
- oasis
- erosion
- butte
- mesa
- spring

What I Do

Complete the Activities. When you are done, you will know about children who go to school outside by a watering hole, which states have the nicknames "Land of Enchantment" and "Natural State," and a gold rush that had a special song written about it.

Name _____ **Date** _____

Activity 1

You are going to make a different kind of map. It is a personal map that will show what you think is important.

Think of five places that are very important to you. On your map, make these places the biggest things on the map. Place them in the correct location relative to one another. Put other landmarks on the map, too. Do not worry about the scale.

Compare your map to your friends' maps. Did you think the same things were important?

_____

_____

Activity 2

Think of the map you made in Activity 1. Now you are going to make another personal map, but this time, you have to draw it from a different **perspective**. When you look at something with a different perspective, you are looking at it from a different **point of view**.

This time, you must take the point of view of an adult. Think of five places that you think are important to an adult and make those places the biggest things on your map.

Contrast this activity's map to Activity 1's map.

Write two sentences about how they are different.

_____

Name _____　　**Date** _____

Activity 3

The Al Murrah are nomads that live in the part of the Arabian Desert known as the Rub' al Khali, or "Great Sandy Desert." They roam over a vast "ocean" of sand where summer daytime temperatures can reach 130°F (54°C).

The Al Murrah herd camels. They live in tents and sit and sleep on rugs that they make. Their main food consists of dates, rice, and camel's milk. The Al Murrah carry water in bags made from goatskin or inner tubes.

Where do Al Murrah children go to school? Schools are set up outside at an **oasis**, or watering hole with vegetation. The school is nothing but a white umbrella and a chalkboard. For entertainment, people sing and recite poetry.

On the map, find and label the Rub' al Khali Desert. It is in the south Arabian Peninsula in Saudi Arabia.

On another sheet of paper, sketch a map from an Al Murrah nomad's perspective. Put five places or things on the map that you think would be important to an Al Murrah person.

Are these the same types of things on your map from Activity 1?

Using a complete sentence, answer the question: What is an oasis? _____

_____

Activity 4

Look at the map. Is the park a good park? It depends on your perspective. Rank the park on a scale from 1 to 5: 1 is the lowest score, 5 is the highest. Rank the park as different people might rank it. Think about what different people want and need, and what they feel is important.

Scores

5th-grade child: _____

teenager: _____

parent: _____

park worker: _____

dog owner: _____

physically-challenged person: _____

Choose three of your scores. Write one sentence for each score. In the sentence, give reasons why that score was given.

1. _____

2. _____

3. _____

Name _____ **Date** _____

Activity 5

Sometimes songs can tell us how people feel. We can use songs to teach history, too. Read the words to the song "Take Me Out to the Ball Game." Jack Norworth wrote these words in 1908:

Take me out to the ball game,
Take me out to the crowd.
Buy me some peanuts and Cracker Jacks,
I don't care if I never come back.

And it's root, root, root for the home team,
If they don't win it's a shame.
For it's one, two, three strikes, "You're out!"
At the old ball game.

The words to the song tell us that the writer

A. was a baseball player

B. did not care which team won

C. liked to go to watch baseball games

D. did not watch baseball on television

How many states would you have to cross if you traveled from where you live in a straight line to the Baseball Hall of Fame in Cooperstown, New York? _____

Activity 6

Baseball is considered to be an American game. People once thought it was invented in 1839 by Abner Doubleday in Cooperstown, New York. It is more likely that it came from an English game called Rounders. Americans changed the rules and made it into the game we have today. The game became popular during the Civil War (1861–1865) among the troops.

On the map, find the countries listed below. Write the sport that originated in that country on the map.

United States—baseball	Canada—ice hockey	England—soccer
India—chess	Scotland—golf	Germany—bowling
Netherlands—speed skating	France—croquet	Japan—karate
Iran (Ancient Persia)—polo	Korea—tae kwon do	Italy (Ancient Rome)—boxing

Name _____ **Date** _____

Activity 7

In 1848, gold was discovered in California near present-day Placerville. The gold rush was on! More than 40,000 gold seekers came in just two years. The song below is about a woman who journeyed from Pike County, Missouri, to Placerville in search of gold. It is called "Sweet Betsy from Pike."

Oh, don't you remember sweet Betsy from Pike,

Who crossed the big mountains with her lover Ike,

With two yoke of oxen and one spotted hog,

A tall Shanghai rooster, and one yellow dog.

From the song, you can tell that Betsy most likely

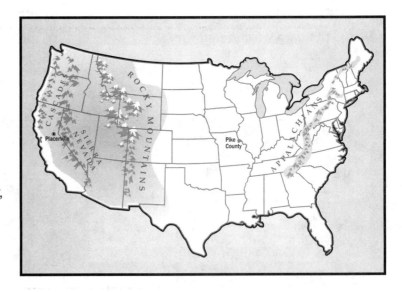

A. did not want to go

B. ate her hog on the way

C. traveled in a covered wagon

D. took the train to California

On the map, trace a line from Pike County, Missouri, to Placerville, California.

Activity 8

Part of the last verse of "Sweet Betsy from Pike" goes:

They swam the wide rivers and crossed the tall peaks,

And camped on the prairie for weeks and for weeks.

From these lyrics, you can tell that

A. the trip to California was short

B. Betsy liked the trip to California

C. people had enough food on the trip

D. the trip to California was not easy

Circle two mountain ranges Betsy most likely crossed:

Rockies   Appalachian   Sierra Nevada

Circle two states with prairies:

Utah   Kansas   Nebraska

Why was it difficult for Betsy to cross rivers? _____

Name _____ **Date** _____

Activity 9

There is more than one famous gold rush. The following are some famous gold rushes:

Placerville, California 1848   Witwaterstrand, South Africa 1884

Australia 1851–1853   Klondike, Canada 1897–1898

Gold is still being mined today. The following were the top producers of gold in 2004:

   1. South Africa   **2.** Australia   **3.** United States   **4.** China   **5.** Russia

On the map, mark the past gold-rush sites and the top gold-producing countries in 2004. Add a key to the map that explains which symbol or color you used for gold-rush sites and top gold-producing countries of 2004.

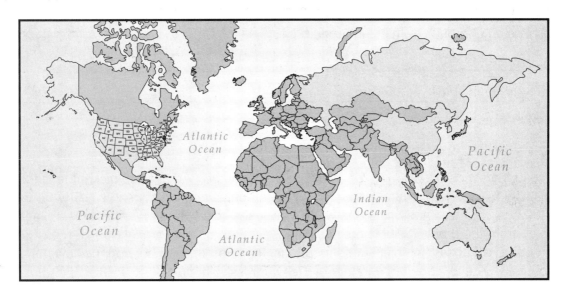

Activity 10

All the states in the United States have a nickname. New Mexico's nickname is "Land of Enchantment." The nickname helps you feel a certain way about the state. When something is enchanting, it is charming and delightful.

The nickname may have been chosen to help people focus on the state's

   A. border of Mexico   **C.** growing more chili peppers than any other state

   B. colorful landscapes   **D.** being the test site of the first U.S. atomic bomb

Find New Mexico on the map. Which direction is it from where you live? _____

New Mexico contains an area called the "Four Corners." What other three states can you stand in while standing in New Mexico? _____

What is your state's nickname? Do you think it is a good nickname? Why or why not?

_____

Name _____ **Date** _____

Activity 11

Long ago, ancient sea floors were uplifted and volcanoes erupted. Then millions of years of erosion took place. **Erosion** is when something is worn away by wind or water. It was these forces of nature that helped shape New Mexico's enchanting landscapes.

Two physical landforms New Mexico is known for are buttes and mesas. A **butte** is a hill with a flat top that is formed when hard rock on the surface protects softer soil underneath it from being eroded. A butte is often steep-sided and seems to rise abruptly from the surrounding area. A **mesa** is a hill or mountain with a flat top that has one or more steep or cliff-like sides. A mesa is larger than a butte.

Write the word *butte* or *mesa* under the corresponding picture.

What keeps the top of a butte from being eroded?

_____

_____

Activity 12

When you read the words *natural wonders*, what do you think of? Arkansas's nickname is the "Natural State." Arkansas is filled with natural wonders. It has the only diamond mine in North America that is open to the public. It also has one of the world's largest single springs. A **spring** is a place where water flows up from the ground. At Mammoth Spring, nine million gallons (34,069 kL) flow from the spring in an hour! Arkansas has plenty of hot springs, too. Forty-seven hot springs flow out of Hot Springs Mountain. The average temperature of the water is a whopping 143°F (62°C)!

Which one of the following refers to a natural wonder?

A. Arkansas elected the first woman to the U.S. Senate in 1932.

B. Arkansas has miles of scenic hiking trails in the Ouachitas Mountains and Ozarks.

Find Arkansas on the map. Which river makes up its eastern border? _____

What are some natural wonders where you live?

_____

_____

_____

_____

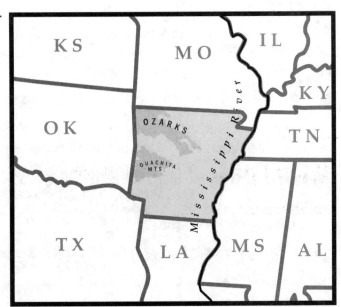

Patterns on Earth's Surface

What I Need to Know

Vocabulary

- hardiness zone
- landform
- peak
- plain
- plateau
- pond
- prairie
- glacier
- aquifer
- volcanic vent

About Patterns on Earth's Surface

A pattern is a habit, a way of acting that does not normally change. Our seasons on Earth form a pattern. The pattern is determined by Earth's tilt. Often, the weather seems to follow a pattern. Weather can, in part, be determined by landforms. Landforms can also determine what or who can live nearby. They help develop community patterns.

What I Do

Complete the Activities. When you are done, you will know about a lake that blew up. You will know about places where there are days that it never grows dark. You will know about a place where there was a 100°F (56°C) temperature change in just one day!

Name _____ **Date** _____

Activity 1

The seasons are caused by the Earth tilting on its axis as it orbits the sun. When the Northern Hemisphere is tipped closest to the sun, it is summer there and winter in the Southern Hemisphere. When the Southern Hemisphere is tipped closest to the sun, it is summer there and winter in the Northern Hemisphere.

Make a bigger diagram of the smaller diagram.

On your diagram, write these words at least once:

axis	sun	Northern Hemisphere
equator	Earth	Southern Hemisphere

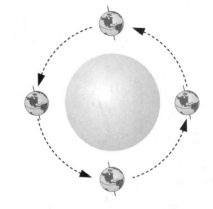

On your diagram, write these words twice:

summer	fall	winter	spring

(Each season word will go once on the Northern Hemisphere and once on the Southern Hemisphere.)

Activity 2

In almost all of the United States, we have daylight savings time. In the spring, we set our clocks one hour ahead, or "spring forward." In the fall, we set our clocks one hour back, or "fall back." Why? We do this so we can have more daylight hours when we are active. We use less energy to light and heat our homes if we are active when the sun is up.

What if you lived in the far north or far south? You would have some months with lots of daylight hours, and other months with little or no daylight hours.

Circle the job in each pair that would be most affected by the number of daylight hours:

        mining underground   or   fishing

        logging   or   making computer parts

Should the school calendar be the same for people in the far north and far south as it is for you? Why or why not? If it should be changed, how should it be changed? _____

_____

Would you have a hard time falling asleep if it were light at night? _____

Name _____ **Date** _____

Activity 3

What causes the seasons? _____

Answer *true* or *false.*

_____ **1.** When it is summer in the Northern Hemisphere, it is winter in the Southern Hemisphere.

_____ **2.** Both the Northern and Southern Hemispheres tilt toward the sun at the same time.

_____ **3.** In the Southern Hemisphere, fall comes after winter.

_____ **4.** Spring is longer in the Northern Hemisphere.

Use the map to help answer the questions.

When it is winter in Canada, it is summer in

  A. Argentina   **B.** Mexico

When it is spring in Zambia, it is fall in

  A. Tanzania   **B.** Poland

January is a winter month in the United States.
January is a summer month in

  A. China   **B.** Australia

July is a summer month in India.
July is a winter month in

  A. Uruguay   **B.** France

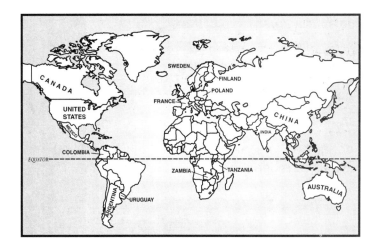

Activity 4

Daylight hours are due to Earth's rotating and tilting on its axis. Remember that the poles tilt away from or toward the sun, depending on the time of the year. If a pole is closer to the sun, the tilt of the Earth is such that the sun never sets. There is daylight all day and night. If a pole is farther away from the sun, the tilt of the Earth is such that the sun never rises.

If you lived in the far north, you would not see the sun

  A. when the Poles tilt the same toward the sun

  B. when the North Pole is tilting toward the sun

  C. when the South Pole is tilting away from the sun

  D. when the North Pole is tilting away from the sun

One part of the Earth has days about the same length all year round. That part of the Earth is most probably

  A. far from the equator   **C.** close to the prime meridian

  B. close to the equator   **D.** far from the prime meridian

Which country has longer summer daylight hours?

  A. Finland   **B.** United States

Which country has shorter winter daylight hours?

Name _____ **Date** _____

Activity 5

You don't have a giant panda, but just in case one comes around, you want some food for it. You'd look in a garden catalog and find a type of bamboo that giant pandas eat, but how would you know if it will grow where you live?

The United States Department of Agriculture (USDA) has made maps that divide the United States into zones called **hardiness zones**. If something is hardy, it is strong and sturdy. Hardiness zone maps are made to show which plants are hardy enough to live in different zones. The zones show average cold temperatures.

The catalog says that this bamboo grows well in zones 6 through 9. Use the hardiness zone map to find your answer.

Is this type of bamboo hardy enough for where you live? _____

Which state is it more likely to grow best in?

  A. Nebraska   **B.** South Carolina

For bamboo to grow, what other things might you have to consider besides hardiness zones?

_____

_____

_____

Activity 6

Find and label Nevada and Kansas on the USDA hardiness zone map below.

If one of the two states planted mostly one crop, that state would most likely be _____ .

One of these states produces more wheat than any other state. It is most likely _____ .

These maps (do/do not) show you how much water there is.

These maps (do/do not) show the kind of soil there is.

Tornadoes twist across one state. Can you tell which state from the map? yes/no

Generally, one would expect states

  A. east and west of a certain state to have different zones

  B. north and south of a certain state to have different zones

Why? _____

_____

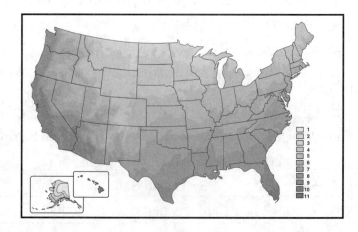

Name _____ **Date** _____

Activity 7

Landforms are natural features on Earth's surface. Practice using these landform words. On another sheet of paper, draw and label a picture of each landform.

peak: the highest point of a mountain

peninsula: a piece of land that juts into a body of water that is surrounded by water on three sides

plain: a nearly flat region of land

plateau: a large, mostly level area of land that stands higher than the surrounding area and is larger than a butte

pond: a small body of fresh water

prairie: a treeless plain, usually covered by tall grass

   Should you have your peninsula surrounded by water on three sides?   yes/no

   Should you make a peak on your plateau?   yes/no

   Should you put trees on your picture of the prairie?   yes/no

Activity 8

A **glacier** is a thick bed of ice formed in Polar Regions or on high mountains. For a glacier to form, more snow has to fall than melt. Over the years, the snow gets deeper and deeper. The weight of the top snow presses down on the bottom, and the bottom snow turns into sheets of ice. The ice sheets flow like slow-moving rivers. As glaciers move downhill, they cut sharp cliffs into mountain valleys and carve out holes. They push rocks and dirt ahead of them. When the glaciers retreat, holes and mounds of dirt are left. Glaciers formed many of the lakes we see today.

Mrs. Jones told her class, "The top part of Canada is in the United States." Why? Long ago, glaciers

  A. formed the Great Lakes

  B. formed when more snow fell than melted

  C. in Canada cut sharp cliffs into mountain valleys

  D. pushed the top soil of Canada into the United States

Snow falls in Iowa today. Why don't glaciers form there?

_____

_____

_____

Name _____ **Date** _____

Activity 9

Temperatures vary, or change, more in the middle of continents than they do near oceans. Oceans heat up more slowly than land masses. They cool down more slowly, too.

In summer the ocean is cooler than the land,

    A. so cooler water cools the air that moves from the ocean to the land

    B. so warmer water warms the air that moves from the ocean to the land

In winter, the ocean water is warmer than the land. This means that the warmer water

    A. cools the air that moves from the ocean to the land

    B. warms the air that moves from the ocean to the land

With the ocean's cooling and warming effect, coastal temperatures

    A. vary more than the middle of continents

    B. vary less than the middle of continents

Think about the temperature where you live. Describe winter and summer temperatures. Describe today's temperature, too. _____

_____

Are there any large bodies of water near you that affect your temperatures? _____

Activity 10

There is a temperature record held by Browning, Montana. It is not for the hottest or coldest temperatures. It is for the greatest range of temperatures over a 24-hour period. The record event took place January 23–24, 1916. The day's low was below freezing at -56°F (-49°C). Then, it warmed up to a high of 44°F (7°C). This means that in one day, the temperature changed by 100°F (56°C)!

From the record, you can tell that it is most likely that

    A. Browning, Montana, is by an ocean

    B. Browning, Montana, is near a glacier

    C. Browning, Montana, is by a large body of water

    D. Browning, Montana, is in the middle of a continent

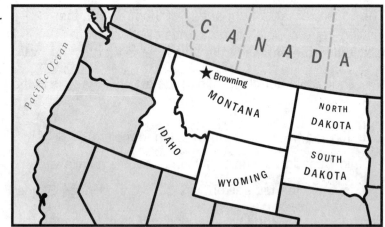

Find Montana on the map. Browning is in the northwestern part of the state. This means that Browning is closer to

    A. Idaho

    B. Wyoming

    C. South Dakota

    D. North Dakota

Why would Hawaii have less varied weather than Montana? _____

Name _____ **Date** _____

Activity 11

Follow the directions below to create a diagram of the water cycle.

1. Draw a lake and an ocean.

2. Draw a river or two that empties into the ocean and/or lake.

3. Draw an aquifer. (An **aquifer** is a water-filled layer of rock, sand, or gravel under the ground.)

4. Draw a pipe that goes down into the aquifer and brings water up to irrigate a field.

5. Over half of the drawing, draw the sun.

6. Write *evaporate* over some water, and draw an arrow from the body of water up into the air toward the sun.

7. Over the other half of the drawing, draw a cloud.

8. Show rainwater falling to the ground.

Activity 12

Sometimes your clothes shrink when you wash them in hot water. Water can shrink a mountain, too! Rainwater can slowly erode the mountain and wear it down, carrying away dirt. If there are not enough plants to hold down the soil, rainwater can cause mudslides, in which big areas of the earth can quickly slide down the mountain.

Water can seep into tiny cracks and freeze. Remember that water expands, or gets bigger, when it freezes. The frozen water fills a crack and pushes against it. It makes the crack bigger. Then, the water thaws and melts, leaving the crack even bigger than before. This can happen again and again. Each time, the crack gets bigger and pieces of rock begin to fall off.

Some mudslides can be prevented by

   A. rainwater running down a mountain

   B. planting trees to hold down the soil

Freezing and thawing water can

   A. cause a mudslide

   B. cause pieces of a rock to fall off over time

A brown river may be a sign of

   A. water freezing and thawing

   B. water carrying dirt down a mountain

Name _____ **Date** _____

Activity 13

Believe it or not, a lake blew up! Lake Nyos in Cameroon exploded in 1986. Eighteen hundred people were killed. How could this happen?

The lake sits on top of a **volcanic vent**. A vent is an opening or passage for something such as air, gas, or molten rock to pass through or escape. A volcano is an opening in Earth's crust in which molten rocks erupt. Often, rocks form a mountain around the opening.

Over time, gasses seeped from the vent into the lake and built up. Finally, they exploded. Water and poisonous gases filled the air. Today scientists are working on a way to stop the lake from exploding again.

Find Cameroon on the map.

Which ocean does Cameroon border? _____

Circle the hemispheres Cameroon is in:

Northern   Southern

Eastern   Western

Are winter days in Cameroon about the same length as summer days? Why or why not?

_____

_____

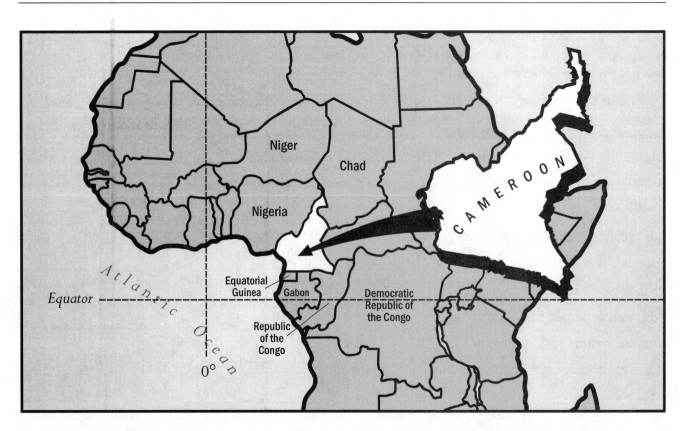

Where Animals and Plants Are Found

About Animals and Plants

Many different animals and plants live on Earth. They make up parts of different ecosystems. In an ecosystem, animals and plants are linked to one another and the land in a special way. Sometimes people can change ecosystems. The changes may mean that some animals disappear or become extinct.

What I Need to Know

Vocabulary

- ecosystem
- canopy
- food chain
- food web
- extinct

What I Do

Complete the Activities. When you are done, you will know about fish that attach themselves to sharks, a spider that eats birds, and how some snakes trick frogs. You will also know what one man did when he was squeezed by a 10-foot (3 m) boa constrictor.

Name _____ **Date** _____

Activity 1

In 1820, Charles Waterton went to Guyana. He wanted to bring new animals back to England. He saw a snake. It was a 10-foot (3 m) boa constrictor. The snake hissed angrily at him. There was not a minute to be lost. Waterton put his hand in his hat. Then, he drove his hat-covered fist right into the snake's jaws! How did Waterton get the snake to his camp? He let the stunned snake coil himself around his body! Waterton wrote, "He pressed me hard, but not alarmingly so."

Snakes live on every continent but Antarctica. However, the same kinds of snakes do not live on every continent. This is because different types of snakes live in different vegetative and climate zones.

The boa constrictor Waterton brought back most likely lived in what type of zone?

A. tundra

B. hot desert

C. tropical rain forest

D. cool or boreal forest

Find Guyana on the map.

What direction is Guyana from where you live? _____

Guyana's neighbor to the west is _____ .

Activity 2

There are more than 2,700 different kinds of snakes. All snakes are part of **ecosystems**. There are different ecosystems all over the world. In each ecosystem, plants and animals are linked to one another and the land in a special way.

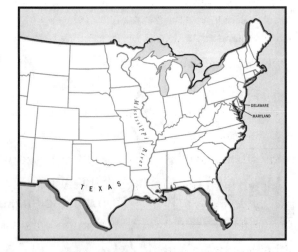

The southern copperhead uses a trick to attract its prey: it wriggles its bright yellow tail to hold a frog's attention. While the frog's attention is on the snake's tail, the snake gets ready and moves its front end into position to strike.

From the story, you can tell that

A. all snakes eat frogs

B. most snakes have tricks to attract prey

C. the frog and the snake are part of the same ecosystem

D. there are more than 2,700 different kinds of ecosystems

The southern copperhead has been found from south Delaware and Maryland down the East Coast and across to Texas. Have the snakes been found on both sides of the Mississippi River?

Name _____ **Date** _____

Activity 3

Marine ecosystems are water ecosystems. There are saltwater, freshwater, river, and tidal marine ecosystems.

Most sharks are part of saltwater ecosystems. They eat fish and marine animals. There is one kind of fish that sharks are linked to in a "friendly" way. It is called a remora.

Remoras have special suckers that they use to attach themselves to a shark's skin. They clean the shark's skin with their mouths. What do they get for their work? They get to eat part of what the shark catches.

Which is not part of a marine ecosystem?

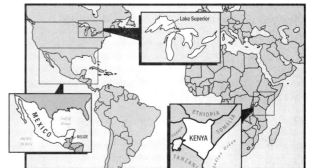

A. a whale that migrates up from Mexico

B. a clam living on a coral reef off of Belize

C. a mussel attached to a ship in Lake Superior

D. an elephant using dust to give himself a bath in Kenya

On the map, find the four places listed in the answers. Which place is farthest east from where you live? _____

Activity 4

One scientist found a new ecosystem in the **canopy** of coastal redwood forests. Canopies are made of tree crowns. The crown is the top branches of the tree. Some coastal redwood trees are almost 2,000 years old. Some are as high as buildings with 37 stories!

High in the canopy, the scientist found new kinds of salamander and earthworm. These animals lived their entire lives above ground. He also found plants that get food and water from air and rain, and trees and shrubs that grow in soil on redwood tree branches.

From the story, you can tell that

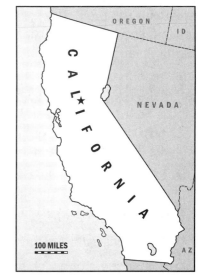

A. all the tree branches make up the tree crown

B. it takes at least 2,000 years for an ecosystem to start

C. canopy ecosystems are only found in coastal redwood trees

D. ecosystems may be different at the top and bottom of trees

Coastal redwoods grow in central and northern California. They are rarely more than 10 miles (16 km) from the coast. Mark on the map where coastal redwoods are found.

What is a tree canopy? _____

_____

_____

Name _____ **Date** _____

Activity 5

Monk parakeets are small birds from South America that were shipped to the United States to be sold as pets. In the 1960s, some escaped from their shipping crates. Over the years, the birds spread. The birds like to build their nests at electric substations and in utility poles. Nests for large flocks can grow as big as a car! The nests have caused fires and the power to go out.

In 2006, people in Texas built platforms that they were hoping would lure, or attract, birds away from the electric substations and utility poles.

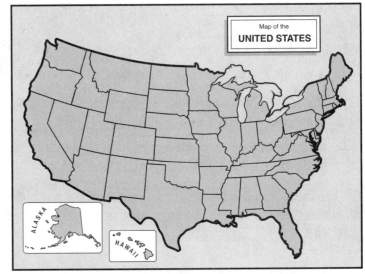

From the story, you can tell that

  A. all utility lines will need to be buried

  B. there are more fires today than in the 1960s

  C. animals brought to new ecosystems may cause changes

  D. monk parakeets would have migrated to the United States

Today, colonies of monk parakeets have been found in Illinois, New York, New Jersey, Florida, Virginia, Washington state, Louisiana, Connecticut, and Texas. Find and label these states on the map.

Count the number of different kinds of birds you see today. Do you think your number will be fewer or more than it would be if you counted the birds at the same place 50 years ago? _____

Activity 6

The world's biggest spider is the goliath bird-eating spider. It can measure up to 11 inches (28 cm) across. (This measurement includes its legs.) The spider has fangs that are used to inject venom into its prey. The spider eats frogs, bats, rodents, lizards, beetles, and birds. To humans, the spider's bite is no more harmful than a bee sting.

The spider has hair on its legs that is stiff and hard. The spider can make a loud hissing sound when it rubs the hair together that can be heard up to 15 feet (5 m) away! The rubbing also flings the sharp hairs into the air. The flying hair and hissing sound protects the spider from other animals.

This spider is found in the coastal rain forests of northeastern South America. Two countries in which it is likely to be found are

  A. Guyana and Peru   **B.** Ecuador and Colombia

  C. Venezuela and Argentina   **D.** Suriname and French Guyana

On another sheet of paper, draw a spider (with eight legs) as large as the goliath bird-eating spider.

Name _____ **Date** _____

Activity 7

A **food chain** shows how plants and animals are connected. It shows that even though different animals eat different things, plants and animals are all connected.

The food chain helps show us that

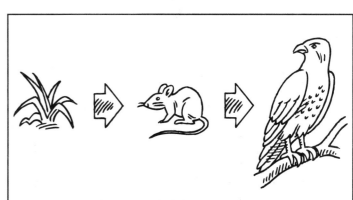

- **A.** hawks only eat mice
- **B.** a hawk is not linked to grass
- **C.** hawks can eat grass if they are starving
- **D.** grass is important to a hawk because it eats animals that eat grass

On another sheet of paper, make two food chains of your own.

1. Put yourself in one of the food chains.

2. Make a food chain for a particular vegetative and climate zone (e.g., tropical rain forest, desert, polar, temperate forest, marine). Write a title for your food chain that includes the name of the zone you are describing.

Activity 8

Sometimes food chains are linked, to make a **food web**. Food webs are another way to show how plants and animals are linked in an ecosystem. Look at the example of the simple food web for a prairie ecosystem.

Make your own food web for a tundra ecosystem. Don't worry if your web has lots of lines going all over the place! Keep these facts in mind as you make your web:

- Some insects eat grass.
- Some insects, such as mosquitoes, suck blood from caribou and people.
- Arctic hares eat grass.
- Some birds eat insects.
- Birds, such as eagles, eat fish.
- People eat hares, caribou, bears, and fish.
- Bears eat fish, berries, and grass.
- Caribou eat grass.
- Wolves eat caribou, hares, birds, and fish.

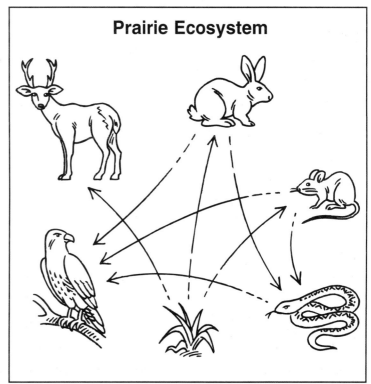

Prairie Ecosystem

Name _____ **Date** _____

Activity 9

What exactly is a tropical rainforest? A tropical rainforest is sometimes called a jungle. It is close to the equator. It is warm all year and has heavy rainfall and a dense, or thick, canopy with many vines.

More species, or kinds, of plants live in tropical rain forest biomes than in any other biome. We get many of our medicines from rainforest plants and many of our foods come from rain forests. For example, we get some of our sugar from rainforest plants in India. There are still many jungle plants and animals we know nothing or little about.

What is not true about a tropical rainforest?

   A. It has a dense canopy.   **C.** It is warmer than any other biome.

   B. It is close to the equator.   **D.** It has more plant species than any other biome.

Today, we get a lot of sugar from sugar cane grown in the West Indies.

Find the West Indies on the map. Draw a line from India to the West Indies.

Name three islands that belong to the West Indies. _____

_____

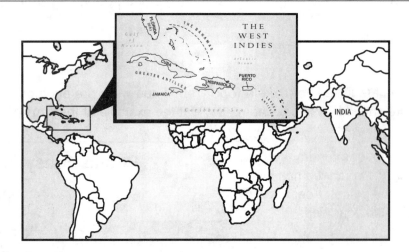

Activity 10

The sad fact is that tropical rainforests are being destroyed faster than any other biome. Trees are being harvested for lumber and land is being cleared for cattle. This ecosystem is being destroyed.

Write *true* or *false* next to each statement below.

_____ Tropical rainforests are being destroyed more slowly than any other biome.

_____ The ecosystem of the tropical rainforests is not affected when trees are cut down.

_____ An ecosystem, such as a tropical rainforest, can be destroyed by human actions.

Think about where you live. Was the land once forested? If it was, how has it changed?

_____

_____

Name _____ **Date** _____

Activity 11

There used to be billions of birds that lived in eastern North America. There were so many of one type of bird that the migrating flocks darkened the sky for days. By 1914, they were **extinct**, which means that they no longer exist and there are no more of its kind left. What kind of bird was it, and what happened to it?

The bird was the passenger pigeon. People began to kill millions of them every year and ship the bodies for meat to city markets by railway carloads. By 1870, the species began to disappear. It became extinct on September 1, 1914, the day when the last passenger pigeon died in a zoo in Cincinnati, Ohio.

How did railroads help the passenger pigeon go extinct?

A. It was a way for people to follow the migrating birds.

B. It was a way to send pigeons quickly to far-away markets.

C. The railway that went through Cincinnati did not stop close to the zoo.

Find Cincinnati, Ohio, on the map. What direction is this location relative to you? _____

About how far is this location from you? _____

Is there at least one state between you and Ohio? If so, name it/them. _____

Activity 12

The passenger pigeon did little damage to crops. Still, it was killed in great numbers for a quick profit. People wanted to make money quickly, so they killed as many birds as they could to sell. The end result was the extinction of the species. Today, people try to conserve, or save, different plant and animal species.

One park in Wisconsin has a monument to the passenger pigeon. The words on the monument say:

"This species became extinct through the avarice and thoughtlessness of man."

Do you agree or disagree? Write three sentences explaining why or why not. (Hint: *Avarice* means "greed.") _____

_____

_____

Find and label Wisconsin on the map. Which state is SW of Wisconsin? _____

Which river and two Great Lakes border Wisconsin? _____

Where People Go

About Where People Go

People come and go, moving to new locations all the time. People may move because they need to find work, or because they think they can have a better life somewhere new. People may move because they have no choice. Physical geography can determine how easy or difficult it is to move. For example, long ago it was hard for people in high mountain valleys to travel freely; it was more common for them to stay in one place than to move about.

What I Need to Know

Vocabulary

- dialect
- census
- urban
- rural
- suburbs
- immigrant

What I Do

Complete the Activities. When you are done, you will know about an island known as "The Island of Hope," which states have the most people, and which states are the most crowded. You will also know if a higher percentage of people can read in Niger than in the United States.

Name _____ Date _____

Activity 1

The Alps divide northern and southern mainland Europe. They stretch about 750 miles (1,207 km) from southeastern France into Slovenia and run through Italy, Switzerland, Liechtenstein, and Austria.

People settled in mountain valleys all across the Alps and developed their own traditions, languages, and dialects. A **dialect** is a form of a language that is used in a certain place or in a certain group.

Why did so many languages and dialects develop? Why wasn't one main language spoken in all the Alpine valleys?

A. Today roads have been built, opening up the valleys.

B. Winter used to be a quiet time, but now tourists come to ski.

C. The mountains acted as barriers and stopped people from moving easily.

D. People moved their cows to higher pastures in the summer months.

On the map, find the Alps and write in the names of the six countries through which they run.

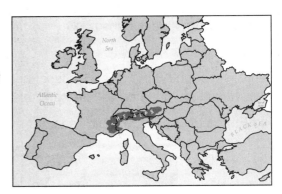

Activity 2

The population is the total number of people who live in a certain place. A **census** is a count of the population. In the United States, a census is taken every 10 years. The first census was taken in 1790.

Look at the census data below. It tells us what the population was in the United States. Make a line graph using the data. Show how the population has changed.

1800—5,308,483 (5 million)

1850—23,191,876 (23 million)

1900—76,212,168 (76 million)

1950—151,325,798 (151 million)

2000—281,421,906 (281 million)

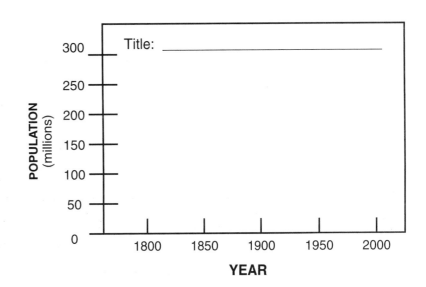

Use the graph to predict. Do you think the population in 2050 will go up or down? _____

How does knowing what to expect help you plan for the future? _____

Name _____   **Date** _____

Activity 3

Take a census in your class. On a separate piece of paper, create a table, chart, or graph to show the data you collected as answers to these questions:

- How many brothers and sisters do you have?
- How many miles do you travel to school?
- Where were you born?
- What month were you born?

- What is your favorite sport?
- What are the ages of your parents?
- What are the ages of your grandparents?
- What language do you speak at home?

Think about your class census. Do you think the following groups would answer in the same way?

- a class in another city
- a class in another state
- a class in Eritrea

Eritrea is a country that gained independence in 1993. In 2005, about 70 out of every 100 people survived on food donated by international organizations. About 60 percent of adults could read.

Find Eritrea on the map. Which sea does it border? _____

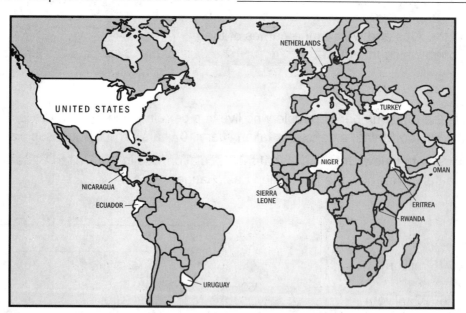

Activity 4

The United States is known for its schools and its education. Many people come to the United States because they want to make better lives for themselves and their children. People who are educated tend to be more successful; they find it easier to get work and earn money.

On another sheet of paper, make a bar graph showing the literacy rates of the countries below. The literacy rate tells how many adults can read out of every 100 in that country's population.

United States—97%	Netherlands—99%	Nicaragua—68%	Ecuador—93%
Niger—18%	Oman—76%	Rwanda—70%	
Sierra Leone—31%	Turkey—87%	Uruguay—98%	

Which countries do you think are the wealthiest—those with high or low literacy rates? _____

On the map, find the countries listed above.

Name _____ **Date** _____

Activity 5

The population of the United States is not evenly distributed. The population is greater in some states than in others. In 2004, this is how the states were ranked for population.

Rank	State	Rank	State	Rank	State
1	California	31	Mississippi	41	New Hampshire
2	Texas	32	Arkansas	42	Hawaii
3	New York	33	Kansas	43	Rhode Island
4	Florida	34	Utah	44	Montana
5	Illinois	35	Nevada	45	Delaware
6	Pennsylvania	36	New Mexico	46	South Dakota
7	Ohio	37	West Virginia	47	Alaska
8	Michigan	38	Nebraska	48	North Dakota
9	Georgia	39	Idaho	49	Vermont
10	New Jersey	40	Maine	50	Wyoming
11	North Carolina				
12	Virginia				
13	Massachusetts				
14	Indiana				
15	Washington				
16	Tennessee				
17	Missouri				
18	Arizona				
19	Maryland				
20	Wisconsin				
21	Minnesota				
22	Colorado				
23	Alabama				
24	Louisiana				
25	South Carolina				
26	Kentucky				
27	Oregon				
28	Oklahoma				
29	Connecticut				
30	Iowa				

On the map, write the number the state was ranked for population in its outline.

Name _____ **Date** _____

Activity 6

In Activity 5, you ranked the states by population. Density is how thick or crowded something is. The density of a state is how many people live per square mile of land area in that state.

Rank	State	Rank	State	Rank	State
1	New Jersey	18	Georgia	35	Oklahoma
2	Rhode Island	19	Tennessee	36	Arizona
3	Massachusetts	20	New Hampshire	37	Colorado
4	Connecticut	21	South Carolina	38	Maine
5	Maryland	22	Louisiana	39	Oregon
6	New York	23	Kentucky	40	Kansas
7	Delaware	24	Wisconsin	41	Utah
8	Florida	25	Washington	42	Nebraska
9	Ohio	26	Alabama	43	Nevada
10	Pennsylvania	27	Missouri	44	Idaho
11	Illinois	28	Texas	45	New Mexico
12	California	29	West Virginia	46	South Dakota
13	Hawaii	30	Vermont	47	North Dakota
14	Virginia	31	Minnesota	48	Montana
15	Michigan	32	Mississippi	49	Wyoming
16	Indiana	33	Iowa	50	Alaska
17	North Carolina	34	Arkansas		

On the map, write the number the state was ranked for density in its outline.

Look at the maps from Activities 5 and 6 to help you answer the questions. On the map, write the number the state was ranked for density in its outline.

If a state is big in size, must it always have a large population? _____

Name a state that supports your answer.

_____

Are states with the greatest population density most likely east or west of the Mississippi?

_____

Name a state that supports your answer.

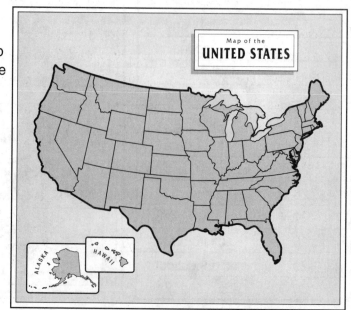

Name _____ Date _____

Activity 7

Even within a state, the population density varies from place to place. An **urban** area is a city or town. A **rural** area is made up of farmland or countryside.

Think about where you live. Where do most of the people live?

   A. urban areas   **B.** rural areas

Name some of the biggest cities in your state. _____

On another sheet of paper, sketch a map of your state. Mark the cities on the map.

Now think about where people live in cities. Do they live close to or far away from downtown?

   A. close   **B.** far away

One reason people may want to live close to the main part of the city is because

   A. it is far away from work   **B.** it is close to work

Today, many people have moved to the suburbs. A **suburb** is a place where people live on the outskirts of a city or town.

Why are the suburbs fairly new in the course of history?

   A. The cities became too crowded.

   B. Cars, buses, and trains were invented so people could get to work quickly.

Activity 8

How does a city begin? Long ago, cities were usually started in a river valley. People could grow more food than they could eat and trade some of their food for other goods. Other people could make things and trade what they made for food. Goods could be traded along the river or along a coast.

Today, many big cities are trade centers, or industrial centers. Industry is any branch of business or manufacturing. When you manufacture something, you make it. Machines are often used to manufacture goods.

On the map, find and label some of the world's biggest cities (see the list below).

Tokyo, Japan	Mumbai (Bombay), India	Mexico City, Mexico
Kolkata (Calcutta), India	New York City, United States	Shanghai, China
Sao Paulo, Brazil	Buenos Aires, Argentina	

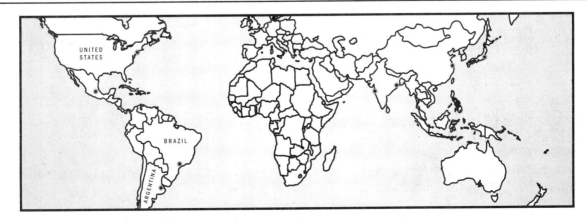

Name _____ **Date** _____

Activity 9

The United States is a nation of **immigrants**. An immigrant is a person who has moved to a new country to make a home. Think about how long you have lived in your current house. Then, think about how long ago your family immigrated to this country.

Write what country or countries your family came from before coming here. _____

On the map, mark some of the places your family came from.

On a separate piece of paper, make two charts for your class. One chart will represent the number of years students have lived in the present location and the other the number of years students' families have been in this country.

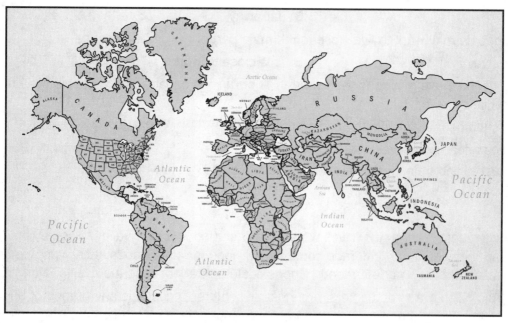

Activity 10

Data is facts or figures from which something can be learned. Look at the data in the table below. Contrast the data. On the back of this paper, write four sentences about how the data are different for each country.

	United States	**Haiti**
Life expectancy (yrs.)	75 male, 81 female	52 male, 54 female
Infant mortality (per 100)	8	74
Urban population	80%	38%
Per capita gross domestic product (GDP)	$40,100	$1,500

Life expectancy is how many years on average a person is expected to live.

Infant mortality is how many children die for every 1,000 live births.

Urban population is how many people live in cities.

Per capita gross domestic product is the average profit on the total of goods and services made per person.

Find the two countries on the map.

Name _____ **Date** _____

Activity 11

When a census is taken, more than just a count takes place. Information about the population is gathered. People are asked how old they are and where they live. They are asked how many children they have and the ages of their children. They are asked what languages they speak and how many years they have lived in the country. They are also asked where they work, how much money they make, and how much education they have.

From the above paragraph, choose three of the questions people are asked when the census is taken. On the back of this paper, write two sentences for each question. In the first sentence, explain why you think this question was asked. In the second sentence, explain how the answer can help a region plan for the future.

Activity 12

Ellis Island is in Upper New York Bay. From 1892–1954, it was an immigrant station. During that time, most immigrants to the U.S. came through Ellis Island. It was known as "The Island of Hope." Today, Ellis Island is a national park.

On another sheet of paper, write a diary entry about Ellis Island. Pretend you are a U.S. immigrant. You might want to mention why you immigrated and what you hope to do in your new country. You can write about how you feel about learning English, too.

Find and circle Ellis Island on the map.

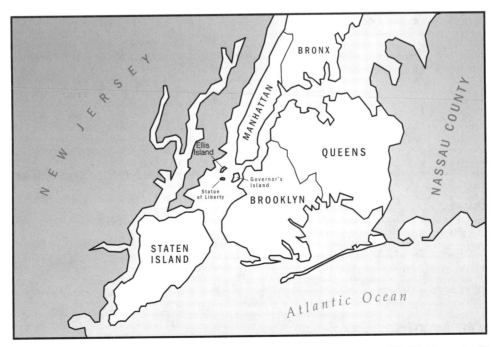

People Patterns

About People Patterns

Different groups of people have different cultures. Culture includes our language, our religion, our arts, how we dress, and what we believe. Different cultures are spread all over the world in a pattern. In today's world, many cultures are changing. As people move, parts of new and old cultures are shared. New patterns are taking shape.

What I Need to Know

Vocabulary

- culture
- sea
- steppe
- crafts

What I Do

Complete the Activities. When you are done, you will know about some people who will not comb their hair indoors, and some people who often had mice living in their hair! You will know where ketchup first came from and why margarine was invented.

Name _____ **Date** _____

Activity 1

Our **culture** is what makes us special. Many things add up to our culture—including our language, our religion, how we dress, how we treat each other, and how we work. Our culture is learned from the people around us. Different people around the world have different cultures.

Describe parts of your culture.

Language: _____

Religion:_____

Dress: _____

Shelter: _____

Education: _____

Customs: _____

Jobs: _____

Activity 2

Where do you comb your hair? Most people comb their hair inside the house. Not so for the Kalash people who live in northwest Pakistan. The women braid their hair in five braids. The middle braid emerges from the middle of their forehead. Kalash women do not braid their hair inside the house, but rather outside near a river. They believe it is bad luck to braid it inside.

If you visit the Kalash, you would want to know their customs because

A. you would want to wear a hat to cover one's hair

B. you would want to bring extra combs to give as gifts

C. you would want to tell the Kalash how they were wrong

D. you would not want to insult the Kalash without meaning to

Find Pakistan on the map. Mark the northwest part.

Pakistan borders a sea. A **sea** is a large body of salt water surrounded partly by or next to land.

Which sea does Pakistan border? Of which ocean is the sea a part?

Name _____ **Date** _____

Activity 3

Most people in Pakistan are Muslims. Muslims believe in Islam, a form of religion. The Kalash believe they are descended from Alexander the Great, who passed through northwest Pakistan around 400 BCE. The Kalash are not Muslims. They believe in a religion much like the Ancient Greek religion. Think about religion for a moment. Religion is part of our culture. Most people in the world belong to a religion. Complete the pie chart below by writing the name of the religion by the correct percentage.

Buddhist:	6
Christian:	32
Confucianism and other global religions:	2
Folk religions such as Shamanists and animists:	12
Hindu:	13
Jewish:	1
Muslim:	19
Non-religious/other:	15

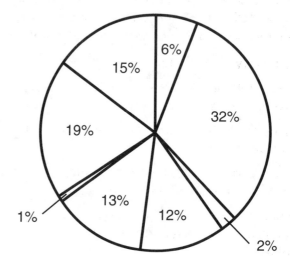

Activity 4

In the 1700s, many French women wore their hair up in high, towering headdresses. It took a lot of time and money to make the headdresses. They were made of wire, cotton padding, and cushions of horsehair. Extra human hair, sticky cream, and powder were also used.

The good thing about the headdresses was that they lasted a long time. The bad thing was that mice and bugs often lived in them! Still, the women wanted to be in fashion. They would carry pretty wands that they could slide into their hair to scratch without ruining their headdresses.

How we dress is part of our culture. From the passage above, we can tell that

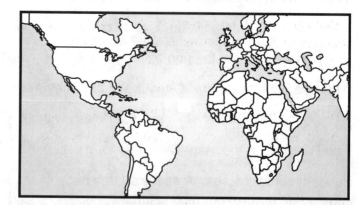

- **A.** a culture never changes
- **B.** fashions are the same in every culture
- **C.** cultures all around the world are the same
- **D.** a culture may have different values at different times

Find and mark France on the map. Which sea and ocean does France border?

_____

Which direction is France from Pakistan? _____

Which direction is France from where you live? _____

Name _____ **Date** _____

Activity 5

Some say ketchup is part of the American food culture. We put it on and in many foods. Where was ketchup invented? What culture was it first part of?

In 1690, the Chinese made a thick sauce of pickled fish and spices called ke-tsiap. This sauce spread to Malaysia, where British sailors brought it back to England in the early 18th century CE. They spelled it *ketchup*. The English tried to make the sauce, but they did not know exactly what was in it. They added salt, cucumbers, walnuts, and even mushrooms. In 1790, people in the United States added tomatoes. Tomatoes soon replaced most everything else.

From the story, you can tell that

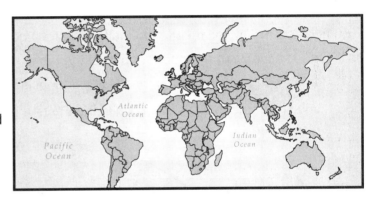

- **A.** people eat the same kinds of food in every culture

- **B.** British sailors brought ketchup to the United States

- **C.** one country's culture may be composed of parts of another culture

- **D.** people in the United States knew what went into ketchup better than the English

On the map, draw arrows from China to Malaysia to England to the United States.

Activity 6

Butter was in such short supply in France in 1869 that a contest was held for a cheap replacement. Only one man entered. He used animal fat, skim milk, pig's stomach, cow's udder, and baking soda. The man called his substance *margarine*, which came from the word *margaron*, the Greek word for "pearl." At one point when the man was mixing his substance, it looked like a string of pearls.

Today, our margarine is made with vegetable fats and vitamins are often added. There is no pig's stomach or cow's udder used. Our margarine was white until the 1950s. There were laws against dying it yellow, because dairy farmers did not want people to think that margarine was butter.

When we think of margarine today, we think of the color yellow because

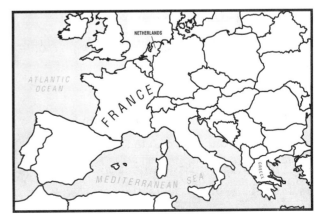

- **A.** we think margarine is butter

- **B.** in Greece, the word *margaron* means yellow

- **C.** dyed margarine has become part of our culture

- **D.** we do not want to think about pig's stomachs or cow's udders

The first margarine factory opened in 1871 in the Netherlands. Find the Netherlands on the map. Which direction are France and Greece from the Netherlands? _____

Name _____ **Date** _____

Activity 7

Horses are an important part of the Mongol culture both in the past and they still are today. Mongols live in Mongolia on a steppe. **Steppes** are vast, treeless plains and are found in southeastern Europe and Asia.

The Mongols invented something in the 2nd century BCE that helped them become expert horsemen. It made it so they could stand, turn, and shoot arrows behind them, all while on the horse. What was it? It was the stirrup!

From the story, you can tell that

   A. horses are not important to the Mongol culture today

   B. horses were more important to Mongols in the 2nd century BCE

   C. horses have been an important part of the Mongol culture for a long time

   D. horses would not be as important to the Mongols if they had not invented the stirrup

Find Mongolia on the map. Is Mongolia in the Eastern or Western Hemisphere? _____

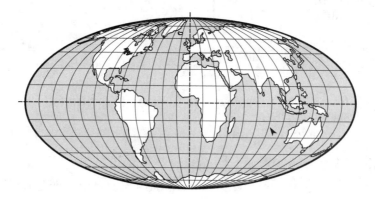

Activity 8

The way a home is built is part of one's culture. Different cultures use different building materials and make a house beautiful in different ways. They build their homes for shelter and to fit the way they live.

Many Mongols are nomads, which means they follow their herds across the steppe. They breed yaks, sheep, camels, and goats. The Mongolian home is a large, white tent called a *ger*. A ger is made of felt, a heavy material made from animal hair pressed tightly together. A ger is always built so its door faces south.

What answer below does *not* explain why Mongols have tent homes?

   A. They are easily taken down.

   B. They can be put up quickly.

   C. They are made from materials at hand.

   D. They can be built with the door facing south.

Go east from Mongolia to where you live. Name a country in between. Do the same going west.

Name _____ **Date** _____

Activity 9

The Sami live in a region of northern Europe known as Lapland. (The Sami are also known as Lapps.) Lapland is within the Arctic Circle, and includes parts of Norway, Sweden, Finland, and Russia. At one time, all the Lapps were nomads. They were reindeer herders.

The Lapps live in an area that is mostly tundra. They wear wool clothes trimmed with reindeer fur. Their clothes are very bright, and their hats are very tall. Sometimes the Sami will stuff their boots or hats with dried grass to help them stay warm.

What might be one reason Sami culture includes brightly-colored clothes?

   A. The clothes help them hide in the reindeer herds.

   B. Brightly-colored clothes are warmer than other clothes.

   C. Children lost on the snowy tundra can be easily spotted.

What might be one reason Sami culture includes tall, bright hats?

   A. The tall hats shade them from the hot sun.

   B. The empty space in the tall hats can be stuffed with dried grass.

   C. The tall hats make them look bigger than the reindeer they are herding.

Find and circle Lapland on the map.

Activity 10

Art is part of every culture. Art includes paintings, sculptures, literature, music, plays, and movies.

The Navajo people are Native Americans. Many Navajo live in Arizona, New Mexico, and Utah. The Navajo are known for their beautiful sand paintings, which are made for special ceremonies. Usually, sand paintings are destroyed soon after they are made, but today some of the designs are saved on special rugs.

The part of the United States many Navajo live in is the

   A. Southwest

   B. Northwest

   C. Southeast

   D. Northeast

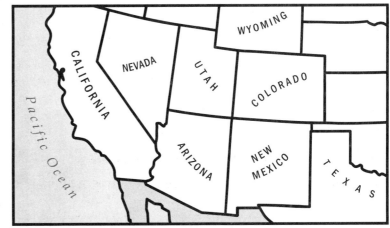

Find and circle the states where many of the Navajo live.

Name _____ **Date** _____

Activity 11

Culture can be reflected in our **crafts**, which are special skills or abilities. Basket-making and weaving are crafts. We refer to many useful items that we use, such as baskets or carved spoons, as crafts.

The Anasazi lived long ago in the area where the states of Arizona, New Mexico, Colorado, and Utah meet. The Anasazi disappeared around 1300 CE, but some of their crafts have survived. Baskets have been found that the Anasazi made to carry water in. To waterproof the baskets, the Anasazi lined them with pinon tree gum. Beautiful pottery has been found, too. Some pieces of pottery had 15 parallel lines in a border less than an inch (2.5 cm) wide!

On another sheet of paper, make a border an inch wide on the bottom or top. Try to make 15 parallel lines in the space. Parallel lines never cross and they stay the same distance apart.

If this is hard for you, think about the Anasazi doing it with paint on curved pottery so long ago!

Find and label on the map where the Anasazi once lived.

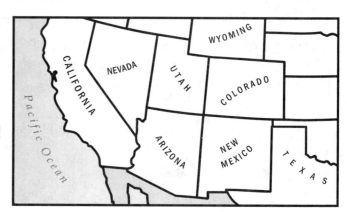

Activity 12

Many people say new inventions change cultures. This does not mean that it is bad to change; it just means that change is a normal part of life.

Choose one of the inventions listed below. Describe three ways this invention has changed your culture. Tell why you think the changes are for the better or worse.

| television | cell phones | cars | computers | Internet |

_____

_____

_____

_____

_____

_____

Buying and Selling Around the World

About Buying and Selling Around the World

All over the world, people buy, sell, and trade goods and services. A good is a thing you can make or sell. Cars, pens, and medicine are goods. A service is work done. You may pay someone to fix something or cook for you. Today, products are sold all over the world. We often buy things made in other countries. Our world has become a global market. Different countries produce different goods that are sold all over the world.

What I Need to Know

Vocabulary

- navigator
- strait
- islet
- port
- exported
- natural resource

What I Do

Complete the Activities. When you are done, you will know about the world's largest coins, how a fruit can be eaten a day before it is picked, and a guide who observed something new about a polar bear.

Name _____ Date _____

Activity 1

The Yapese live in Yap, a country that includes 134 islands. The islands are in the Pacific Ocean in a region called Micronesia. Micronesia is made up of the islands of the west Pacific, east of the Philippines.

Circle on your map the area we mean when we talk about Micronesia.

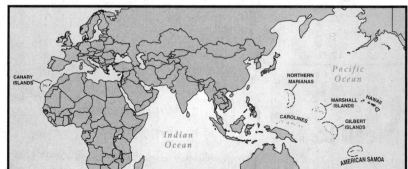

Which islands are not located in Micronesia?

A. Canary Islands

B. Gilbert Islands

C. Marshall Islands

D. Caroline Islands

How do the Yapese support themselves? How do they satisfy their basic needs? Think about where the Yapese live. It is most likely that the main occupations of the Yapese are

A. farming and mining   **C.** mining and forestry

B. fishing and farming   **D.** forestry and manufacturing

Activity 2

The Yapese are some of the Pacific's best **navigators**. A navigator is one who navigates, or guides, and is skilled at finding one's way around.

The Yapese used outrigger canoes to travel from island to island. They used star compasses to navigate the waters. Star compasses were made of stones and leaves. The outer ring of stones showed star constellations and where the constellations rose and set on the horizon. The leaves inside the ring showed the swell of the waves.

Over hundreds of years, the Yapese sailed to volcanic islands over 300 miles (483 km) away. These faraway islands were not part of Yap, but they had money! Yapese coins are the largest coins in the world. The round disks have a hole in the middle, and they are made from volcanic stones. Some of the coins are 12 feet (4 m) tall! The Yapese risked their lives carrying these huge coins on their outrigger canoes back to Yap.

The outer rings of the Yapese's star compasses showed

A. the swell of the waves

B. the location of the Yap islands

C. where the volcanic islands were located

D. where star constellations rose and set on the horizon

Could a Yapese coin fit in your wallet or purse?

_____

Name _____ **Date** _____

Activity 3

The Inuit are native people of the cold North. They live in the Arctic areas of Alaska, Canada, Greenland, and Russia. Traditional Inuit were hunters. They hunted seals, fish, whales, polar bears, and walrus. The Inuit respected the animals they ate. They let nothing of the animal go to waste.

The Inuit made boats called kayaks, which were made with sea mammal skins. The skins were stretched over a light wooden frame. A kayak is different from a canoe. A canoe is open; a kayak is covered, with a hole left open for each passenger.

A kayak might be made differently from a canoe because

- **A.** canoes will not sink if they fill up with water
- **B.** people who make canoes do not have sea mammal skins
- **C.** an Inuit could freeze if soaked with cold Arctic water
- **D.** an Inuit wants to use the entire animal that is caught

On the map, find the areas where the Inuit live. Which sea is between Russia and Alaska?

_____

Activity 4

The Inuit also used dogs for their transportation, having them pull sleds that carried people and supplies. Today, people in the far North often use snowmobiles and boats with motors. To get to many places, they fly in small planes.

Why don't many people drive cars in the far North?

- **A.** Snowmobiles are faster.
- **B.** People do not like to drive.
- **C.** Many of the places do not have roads.
- **D.** It is easier to see where you are going in a plane.

Roger Kuptana is an Inuit guide. In 2006, he tracked a polar bear in the Northwest Territories for a client. Kuptana knew that there was something strange about the bear. Its eyes were ringed with black, its face was slightly indented, it had a mild hump, and it had long claws. DNA tests proved that the bear's mother was a polar bear and its father was a grizzly bear.

Guiding was a good job for Kuptana because it allowed him

- **A.** to earn money doing DNA testing
- **B.** to earn money to move somewhere warm
- **C.** to earn money using his knowledge of the Arctic
- **D.** to earn money for hunting more grizzly bears

Find the Northwest Territories on the map. Which country are they part of? _____

Name _____　Date _____

Activity 5

Think of how roads help us get around. We use roads to transport the food we grow, to bring supplies we need to make things, and to take the finished goods to places where people buy them.

The United States has an interstate highway system. The system is made of highways that link the states together. Construction of these roads began in 1956 and went on for 37 years.

Look at the map to answer the questions.

Even numbered interstate highways run mainly

    A. east to west　　　　　**B.** north to south

Odd numbered interstate highways run mainly

    A. east to west　　　　　**B.** north to south

Which interstate can take you from California to New York?

    A. 80　　　　　　　　　**B.** 81

Activity 6

Water as a form of transportation can help trade. Goods can be carried up and down rivers and across lakes and oceans. However, water can sometimes be a natural barrier. A body of water may take a long time to cross, and it may be difficult to transport items across a river. But if a bridge is built, people and goods can easily move to opposite sides of the water.

One bridge united the cities of Copenhagen and Malmo. The two cities are in different countries, Copenhagen in Denmark and Malmo in Sweden. The bridge opened in 2000, and it is the longest single bridge in the world that has both railroad and road traffic. It is 10 miles (16 km) long.

On the map below, find and label Copenhagen, Denmark. Also find and label Malmo, Sweden.

Which two seas surround Denmark?

_____

Are there any bridges—big or small—near you? How much would you be affected if the bridge(s) disappeared?

_____

_____

_____

_____

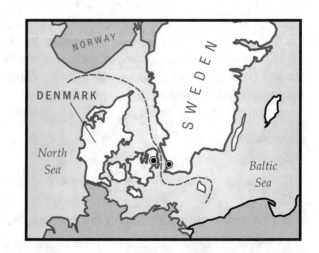

Name _____ **Date** _____

Activity 7

A suspension bridge is a bridge held up by large cables that run between a series of towers. The largest suspension bridge in the world is the Akashi Kaikyo Bridge in Japan. It crosses a **strait**, which is a narrow body of water that connects two larger bodies of water. The Akashi Kaikyo Bridge crosses the Akashi Strait, and it connects the city of Kobe with Awaji Island. The bridge, which opened in 1998, is 2.43 miles (4 km) long.

A

B

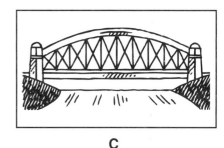

C

Which picture shows a suspension bridge? _____

What is a strait?

_____

_____

_____

Find Japan on the map. Circle Kobe and Awaji Island.

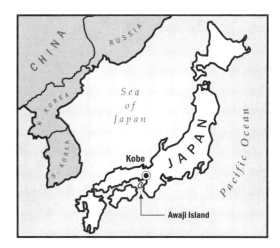

Activity 8

Today, bridges connect all four of Japan's main islands. The designers of the Akashi Kaikyo Bridge had to keep in mind that Japan has many earthquakes. In fact, a huge earthquake hit Kobe in 1995. The designers reinforced the Akashi Kaikyo Bridge with strong, deep foundations. The foundations can withstand earthquakes up to a magnitude of 8.5 on the Richter scale.

The Richter scale is a scale of numbers that represent the relative amount of energy released by an earthquake. The numbers range from 1.0 to 9.0. People may not even feel an earthquake that measures 1.0, but they would strongly feel an earthquake that measures 8.5. Earthquakes of this size can cause a lot of damage. It is not uncommon for buildings to collapse.

Japan probably has many earthquakes because

   A. it crosses a strait   **C.** it is located on the Ring of Fire

   B. it is made up of islands   **D.** it measures a high number of the Richter scale

Which number below shows an earthquake of higher magnitude or strength on the Richter scale?

   A. 2.6   **B.** 6.2

Name _____ **Date** _____

Activity 9

Singapore has one main island and 58 offshore **islets**, which are very small islands. Singapore's port is one of the busiest in the world. A **port** is a harbor or a city with a harbor where ships can load and unload their goods.

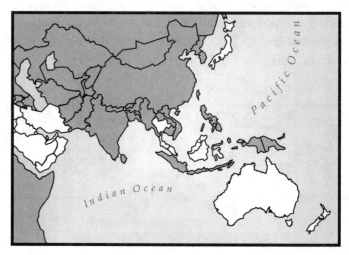

Crude oil is shipped to Singapore, much of which comes from places like Malaysia, Brunei, Indonesia, and the Middle East. Many of Singapore's oil refineries are on its islets. The oil is refined in Singapore into different grades and then sold and exported. When goods are **exported**, they are sent from one country for sale in another. Singapore exports refined oil to Japan, Hong Kong, Malaysia, Australia, Thailand, and many other countries.

What is an islet? _____

_____

What is a port? _____

_____

On the map above, draw arrows from the countries Singapore buys crude oil from to Singapore. Then, draw arrows from Singapore to the countries it sells refined oil to.

Activity 10

A resource is a supply of something. A **natural resource** is a supply that is found in nature and is not man-made. Some natural resources include oil, fish, trees, and good soil.

Many jobs center on natural resources, such as farming, mining, forestry, and fishing. Guiding and service jobs can be centered on natural resources, too. For example, skiing is a tourist industry that exists only where there are mountains and snow. The snowy mountains are a natural resource!

Sketch an outline of your state. Inside the outline, show where some of its natural resources are found.

Name _____ **Date** _____

Activity 11

Jack lives in California and wants some fresh kiwi fruit, so he goes to the store. When he gets there, he says to the store clerk, "I will not buy this kiwi fruit unless it is fresh. Today is February 3. When was this fruit picked?"

The store clerk begins to laugh and says, "You will find this hard to believe, but it is true. This kiwi fruit is from New Zealand and it is very fresh. It fact, it is so fresh that I can honestly say it was picked on February 4!"

If it is February 3 in California, how can this be possible?

   A. New Zealand and California are on the same side of the International Date Line.

   B. New Zealand and California are on different sides of the International Date Line.

On the map, find California, New Zealand, and the International Date Line. Trace the International Date Line.

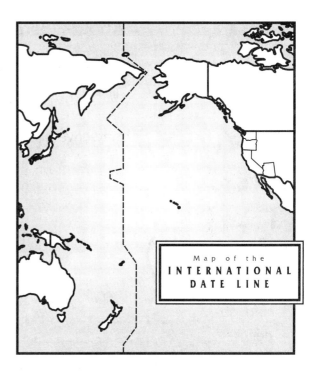

Map of the
**INTERNATIONAL
DATE LINE**

Activity 12

Look again at the International Date Line you found in Activity 11. Places to the east of this line (which are considered in the Western Date) are a calendar day behind places to the west (which are considered in the Eastern Date). If you fly from west to east and cross this line, you go back one day. When it is February 4 in New Zealand, it is February 3 in California. You may leave on a Saturday and arrive in the United States on a Friday. You get to have Saturday all over again! If you fly from east to west and cross this line, you jump ahead one day.

The International Date Line is roughly along the

  A. equator   **B.** prime meridian   **C.** 180° latitude line   **D.** 180° longitude line

The reason the International Date Line is not exactly straight is because it is drawn so

   A. countries in the Northern Hemisphere are all on the same day

   B. one country is not on two different days at the same time

   C. countries that border the Pacific Ocean are all on the same day

   D. one country is not in two different Hemispheres at the same time

Why does an International Date Line help trade?

_____

_____

Where People Settle

About Where People Settle

There are many kinds of settlements around the world. There are different patterns of land use in each settlement that change over time for different reasons. The changes may attract people or they may drive people away.

What I Need to Know

Vocabulary

- refugee
- central business district
- neighborhood
- delta

What I Do

Complete the Activities. When you are done, you will know where some of the tallest buildings in the world are located. You will know about one city that is on two continents and why this city is so important.

Name _____ **Date** _____

Activity 1

Why do you live where you do? List five reasons why your family lives where it does. The following are some things you might want to write about: house size, yard size, schools, cost, location, neighborhood, climate, shopping, and jobs.

1. _____

2. _____

3. _____

4. _____

5. _____

When did your town become a town? Or, when did people first begin to live in your area? Do you think the first settlers lived in your town or area for the same reasons you listed above?

_____

_____

_____

Activity 2

Most people live in cities. People come to cities to find work and a better life. Many cities started where there were natural resources. The soil may have been fertile and good for crops. There may also have been clean water, trees, or minerals to be mined. Jobs developed around the natural resources, and stores and schools were built because of the people. Then new businesses, industries, and manufacturing plants developed.

On the map, find and label some of the biggest U.S. cities listed below.

New York City, New York

Los Angeles, California

Chicago, Illinois

Houston, Texas

Philadelphia, Pennsylvania

Phoenix, Arizona

San Diego, California

San Antonio, Texas

Dallas, Texas

San Jose, California

Which city most likely saw much of its growth after air conditioning was developed?

_____

Name _____ **Date** _____

Activity 3

Read the poems and answer the questions. Both poems are titled "The Skyscraper."

<table>
<tr><td align="center">**POEM A**</td><td align="center">**POEM B**</td></tr>
</table>

POEM A		POEM B	
Built of glass and steel	It is a great mountain,	Built of glass and steel	It is a great cut,
It towers in the sky.	Not of Nature, but of Man.	It slices through the air.	Not of Nature, but of Man.

1. The reader of which poem would most likely want to live in or visit a city?

   A. Poem A   **B.** Poem B

2. Which verb gives a sense of majesty?

   A. towers   **B.** slices

3. Which noun makes you feel something has been harmed?

   A. mountain   **B.** cut

4. Which invention has greatly aided the development of the skyscraper?

   A. the stair   **B.** the elevators

Activity 4

Find and label on the map where some of the world's tallest buildings are. Then answer the questions below.

Building	Location	Height ft (m)
Taipei 101	Taipei, Taiwan	1,670 (509)
Petronas Towers 1 and 2	Kuala Lumpur, Malaysia	1,483 (452)
Sears Tower	Chicago, Illinois, U.S.A.	1,450 (442)
Jin Mao Building	Shanghai, China	1,380 (421)
Two International Finance Centre	Hong Kong, China	1,362 (415)

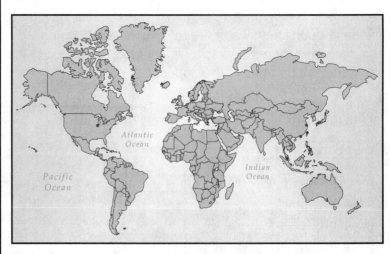

Which building is in the Southern Hemisphere? _____

Which building is in the Western Hemisphere? _____

If it is Sunday at the Sears Tower, what day is it at the Jin Mao Building? _____

To make a skyscraper, a country must have a good supply of _____ .

A country without any big cities is more likely to have a (rural/urban) population.

Name _____ **Date** _____

Activity 5

Antigua and Barbuda were colonized by Great Britain in the 1600s. They became independent in 1981. Most of the people in Antigua and Barbuda are descendents of slaves who were brought to work on sugar plantations.

The sugar-farming industry closed down in the 1970s. Today, most of the people rely on tourism to make a living. Tourists come because of the beautiful beaches and snorkeling and scuba diving. There has also been a big population increase due to **refugees**, people who flee from their homes for safety. Most of the refugees who came were from Montserrat, because they were escaping from an erupting volcano.

From the story, you can tell that

  A. there are no volcanoes on Antigua and Barbuda

  B. some people are forced to leave their settlements

  C. tourism is the best way for a country to make money

  D. the sugar farming industry has closed down everywhere

The United States declared its independence in 1776. About how much longer has it been independent than Antigua and Barbuda?

  A. 205 years   **B.** 281 years

On the map, find Antigua and Barbuda and Montserrat. Which sea do they lie in? _____

Activity 6

Cities are typically divided into areas, including two types of commercial areas. One is the **central business district**, which is often in the center of the city and is the main business area of the city.

The other commercial area is made of big industries. It is often along the outer edges of the city, usually near roads, an airport, railways, and waterways.

One reason the industrial commercial areas are along roads and airports is so

  A. the workers' children can go to school

  B. the airport noise does not bother people

  C. goods and supplies can easily be moved in and out

  D. it is easy for the workers to get downtown

Circle where each building would most likely be found:

main library (downtown/industrial)

wire factory (downtown/industrial)

instrument factory (downtown/industrial)

courthouse (downtown/industrial)

Name _____ **Date** _____

Activity 7

People live in the residential areas of a city. Residential areas are often divided into **neighborhoods**, each with its own make-up. Sometimes people in a neighborhood have the same culture or come from the same background. A neighborhood may be in an old part of town, on a hill, or have a certain physical feature, such as a river.

Many large cities in the United States have "Chinatowns." These places are

    A. a neighborhood on a hill

    B. a neighborhood that is part of China

    C. a neighborhood with a strong Chinese culture and population

    D. a neighborhood in the central business district

What might be a good name for a neighborhood by a river?

    A. Cannery Row   **C.** King's Edge

    B. River's Ridge   **D.** Orchard Heights

Describe your neighborhood. Write at least three sentences. _____

_____

_____

If you could rename your neighborhood, what would you call it? _____

Activity 8

Finish the key for the map below by coloring in the different neighborhoods on the map.

Hint: Suburbs are residential areas just outside a city.

Hint: Industrial areas need to be by major transportation routes.

Key	Color
Downtown Business District	
Industrial Areas	
Residential Areas	
Suburbs	

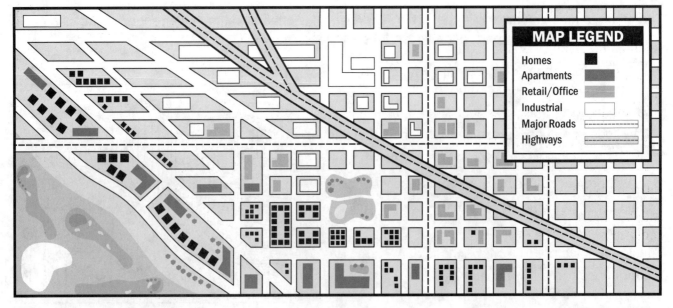

MAP LEGEND

Homes	
Apartments	
Retail/Office	
Industrial	
Major Roads	
Highways	

Name _____ **Date** _____

Activity 9

Sid's parents have decided to move either to Appleville or Orangeville. Sid's father asked to be sent a phone book from both cities. "This will help us decide where we want to move," he said.

Appleville	
13 museums	2 universities
2 hospitals	1 airport
5 elementary schools	104 restaurants
2 high schools	

Orangeville	
1 museum	0 universities
3 doctors	0 airports
1 elementary school	2 restaurants
1 high school	

If Sid's brother needed special medical care, which city would Sid's parent's most likely choose?

_____

Which city is more likely to have a tropical fish store? _____

Which city is more likely to have a mall? _____

Which city is more likely to have a volunteer fire department?_____

Why would you choose Orangeville over Appleville? _____

Why would you choose Appleville over Orangeville? _____

Activity 10

Turkey's largest city is Istanbul. Ancient Greeks founded the city around 660 BCE. It was called Byzantium. In 196 CE, the Romans captured it and renamed it Augusta Antonia. In 330 CE, the name was changed to Constantinople. In 1930, Turkey officially changed the name to Istanbul.

Why is Istanbul such an important city? Why were there so many battles over who controlled it? Its location is very important. It is on both sides of the Strait of Bosporus.

By controlling the city, one controls *access* or a way into and out of

   A. the Black and Red Seas

   B. the Black and Arabian Seas

   C. the Black and Caspian Seas

   D. the Black and Mediterranean Seas

Istanbul lies on two continents! On which two continents does it lie?

_____

_____

Name _____ **Date** _____

Activity 11

Long ago, many people settled along the Nile
River, which is the world's longest river. It flows
northward from Lake Victoria. On the map,
find and label the Nile River and Lake Victoria.

Lake Victoria lies in which three countries?

_____

_____

The Nile River runs through which three
countries into the Mediterranean Sea?

_____

_____

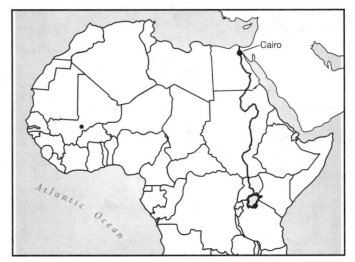

A **delta** is an area of land shaped roughly like
a triangle. It is where a river deposits mud, sand, or pebbles as it enters the sea. The largest city in
Africa lies along the Nile River above the division of two main branches of its delta. What is the name
of the city? _____

What is not true about a delta?

A. It is part of a sea.

B. It is shaped like a triangle.

C. It is where mud, sand, and pebbles are deposited.

Activity 12

One of the oldest cities in Africa is Djenne, which is in Mali. The Great Mosque, the largest mud
building in the world, is in Djenne. It is an Islamic temple that was built in 1907. To make the building,
mud was plastered around a wooden framework. Each spring, the Great Mosque is replastered.

Wooden beams stick out of the Great Mosque high on
the walls. One reason the beams might have been left to
stick out is

A. people did not have saws to cut them

B. people wanted to show off the wood underneath

C. people wanted to use the buildings as a playground

D. people could climb on them when the building
needed to be replastered

Mali lies in part of the largest dry desert in the world. This desert covers about one-third of the
continent of Africa and is getting bigger every year. One reason is that people have used up much of
the plant life that held down the soil. This desert is called the

A. Gobi Desert   **B.** Namib Desert   **C.** Sahara Desert   **D.** Sonoran Desert

On the map above, find and label Djenne, Mali.

How Earth Is Divided Up

What I Need to Know

Vocabulary

- governor
- national government
- bay
- tide
- currency
- civil

About How Earth is Divided Up

People have divided up Earth into countries, each with its own government. A country is divided inside into sections (like states or provinces), and each section has its own government. Inside each section, there are cities and counties, and each of these sections may have its own government.

What I Do

Complete the Activities. When you are done, you will know about a place where water glows in the dark, a place where water flows backward over a waterfall, and a country that was born twice.

Name _____ **Date** _____

Activity 1

The United States is made up of 50 states, each with its own laws and leaders. A state's highest leader is called a **governor**. Each state has a capital city, which is where the state government meets.

All the states have to follow the **national government**. The leader of the national government is the president. The national government meets in Washington, DC, the nation's capital.

On the map, find and label Washington, DC, your state, and your state's capital.

Where is Washington, DC, relative to where you live? Use the map compass and scale to help you give directions and distance.

_____

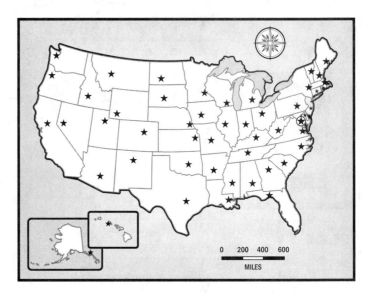

Activity 2

The United States became an independent country in 1776. It was made of 13 states, each being one of the original Thirteen Colonies of Great Britain.

On the map, write the number on each state to tell in which order it became a state. The first state was Delaware. It became a state on December 7, 1787. The last state to join the Union was Hawaii. It became a state on August 21, 1959.

1. Delaware	18. Louisiana	35. West Virginia
2. Pennsylvania	19. Indiana	36. Nevada
3. New Jersey	20. Mississippi	37. Nebraska
4. Georgia	21. Illinois	38. Colorado
5. Connecticut	22. Alabama	39. North Dakota
6. Massachusetts	23. Maine	40. South Dakota
7. Maryland	24. Missouri	41. Montana
8. South Carolina	25. Arkansas	42. Washington
9. New Hampshire	26. Michigan	43. Idaho
10. Virginia	27. Florida	44. Wyoming
11. New York	28. Texas	45. Utah
12. North Carolina	29. Iowa	46. Oklahoma
13. Rhode Island	30. Wisconsin	47. New Mexico
14. Vermont	31. California	48. Arizona
15. Kentucky	32. Minnesota	49. Alaska
16. Tennessee	33. Oregon	50. Hawaii
17. Ohio	34. Kansas	

When did your state become a state? _____

Name _____ **Date** _____

Activity 3

A **bay** is a curved area along a coast or shore where water juts into the land. Bays are usually smaller than gulfs. They have smaller openings, too. In Puerto Rico, there is a special bay that has a small opening. The bay is connected to the ocean with only one narrow channel, so billions of tiny creatures are trapped in the bay. The creatures, called dinoflagellattes, make the water glow—when they are jostled, or bumped, they produce light! Walk through the water, and you will leave a trail of light behind you!

Suppose you were a sailor of long ago and did not know about tiny creatures that could produce light. How might you feel if you entered this bay one night?

    A. angry   **B.** tired   **C.** strong   **D.** fearful

What is a bay?_____

Find Puerto Rico on the map. Is it in the same ocean as Hawaii? _____

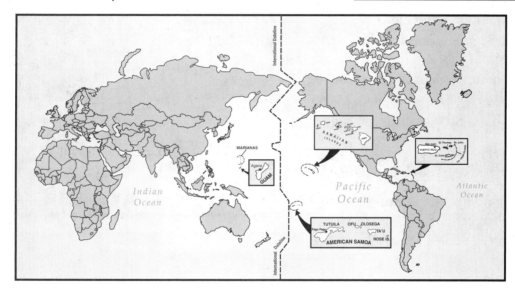

Activity 4

Puerto Rico is part of the United States. It is a territory, not a state. Long ago, it belonged to Spain, and became part of the United States in 1898 after the Spanish-American War.

The United States has other territories, too. They are tropical islands. Puerto Rico, the U.S. Virgin Islands, the Northern Marianas, Guam, and American Samoa are all U.S. territories.

On the map, find Puerto Rico, the U.S. Virgin Islands, the Northern Marianas, Guam, and American Samoa.

Which three are in the Pacific Ocean?

    A. American Samoa, Puerto Rico, Guam   **C.** U.S. Virgin Islands, Guam, Northern Marianas

    B. Guam, Northern Marianas, American Samoa   **D.** Northern Marianas, American Samoa, U.S. Virgin Islands

If it is Sunday in Puerto Rico, it is _____ in Guam.

    A. Sunday   **B.** Monday   **C.** Tuesday   **D.** Wednesday

Name _____ **Date** _____

Activity 5

On the line, write *north, south, east,* or *west.* Canada is the United States' neighbor to the _____.

Canada is divided into provinces and territories. On the map, fill in the names using the clues.

Saskatchewan—north of Montana and
  North Dakota

Yukon Territory—shares border with Alaska

British Columbia—borders the Pacific Ocean

Northwest Territories—east of Yukon, north
  of Saskatchewan

Nova Scotia—peninsula in Atlantic Ocean,
  close to Maine

Quebec—west of Newfoundland and
  Labrador, north of Vermont

Alberta—in between British Columbia and
  Saskatchewan

Nunavut—north of Manitoba and Quebec

New Brunswick—borders eastern Maine

Manitoba—east of Saskatchewan, west of
  Ontario

Ontario—part of Lake Superior is in this
  province

Newfoundland and Labrador—borders
  Atlantic Ocean

Prince Edward Island—in Atlantic Ocean,
  smallest province

Activity 6

Canada's Bay of Fundy is a natural wonder. The highest tides in the world occur in the Bay of Fundy. A **tide** is a change in the level of an ocean or sea, which happens primarily because of the pull of gravity between Earth and the moon. High tide happens twice daily.

In the Bay of Fundy, tides rise and fall as much as 50 feet (15 m)! One can see the tide come in as a wall of water about 2 feet (61 cm) high that rushes into the Petitcodiac River. It also runs into the St. John River, making the water in the river rise so much that the river becomes higher than the Reversing Falls of St. John and runs backward up and over them!

One word in each sentence is incorrect. Change the word.

  1. A tide is a change in the level of an ocean or a lake.

  2. A tide is due primarily to the pull of gravity between the water and the moon.

  3. High tide happens once daily.

  4. It is impossible for a tide to make water run backward over a fall.

On the map above, find and label the Bay of Fundy. It lies between Nova Scotia and New Brunswick.

Name _____ **Date** _____

Activity 7

Each state has its own leaders, nickname, capital, and flag. Each state even has its own bird and plant. Fill in the blanks below with information about your state. Sketch your state's flag.

Governor's Name	
State Nickname	
State Capital	
State Bird	
State Plant	

Activity 8

Every country has a capital.

The capital of Australia is Canberra. The name comes from an Aborigine word meaning "meeting place." (Aborigines were the first people to live in Australia.)

The capital of Canada is Ottawa. The name comes from an Algonquin Native American word meaning "to trade."

The capital of Zimbabwe is Harare. Harare was an African ruler whose name means "one who does not sleep."

The capital of Thailand is Bangkok. It is named for a Thai word that means "heavenly city."

The capital of Ireland is Dublin. The name comes from the Gaelic words for "black pool." The name refers to the Liffey River that runs through the city.

Find and label each of these capitals on the map. Next to the name, write which direction each capital is from your country's capital.

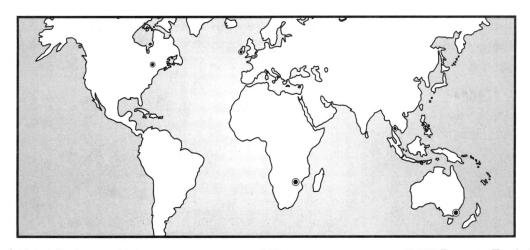

Name _____ **Date** _____

Activity 9

In January 1999, some countries began using a new **currency**, or money in common use. Currency is legal coins and bills. The new currency began to replace the old currency. By February 2002, only the new currency was being used.

The new currency was the Euro. Look at Europe on the map and you will see that it has many countries. Each country had its own currency and trading partners, making it hard for goods to pass freely across borders. Then some of the countries joined together and became the European Union. They became trading partners and allowed goods to go freely across borders. Using a common currency made things easier. Not all of the countries use the Euro.

Why would using a common currency make trading easier?

A. Every country could use its own currency.

B. A common currency is worth a different amount in every country.

C. It makes it hard for people to know how much they are paying for something.

D. People do not have to exchange money every time a border is crossed.

What currency is used in your country? _____

How many Euros are worth one U.S. dollar? (Hint: It changes every day. Check the newspaper or Internet or call a bank to find out.) _____

Activity 10

As of September 25, 2005, the European Union had 25 members. Using the information below, color the 12 original members on the map using one color. Color the next three joining members using another color. Then color the newest members using a third color.

12 original members: Belgium, Denmark, France, Germany, Greece, Ireland, Italy, Luxembourg, the Netherlands, Portugal, Spain, and Great Britain. (Great Britain is made up of England, Scotland, Wales, and Northern Ireland.)

Entered January 1, 1995: Austria, Finland, Sweden

Entered May 1, 2004: Cyprus, Czech Republic, Estonia, Hungary, Latvia, Lithuania, Malta, Poland, Slovakia, Slovenia

Name _____ **Date** _____

Activity 11

What is Oceania? Oceania is made of Australia, New Zealand, Papua New Guinea, and thousands of islands in the Pacific Ocean. The area of Oceania is larger than Asia, but the land mass of Oceania is smaller than Europe.

The Huli people live in Oceania in the central mountains of Papua New Guinea. They live in the rain forest, which is so dense or thick with trees, that no outsider knew the Huli existed until the 1930s!

The Huli live in small, scattered settlements, with each settlement having its own plot of land. Taro and sweet potatoes are grown on the land. Men and women live in different houses, and pigs are their most valuable possessions.

What is not true about Oceania?

A. The area is larger than Asia.

B. The land mass is smaller than Europe.

C. Australia is the only continent in Oceania.

D. Thousands of islands in the Atlantic Ocean are part of Oceania.

On the map, find the places listed above in Oceania. Write the name of three islands or island groups.

_____

_____

Activity 12

Pitcairn Island is in Oceania. It is about halfway between South America and Australia. Philip Carteret discovered Pitcairn Island in 1767, but no one lived there until 23 years later. The people who lived on it did not want to be found because they were mutineers, which means they had committed mutiny. *Mutiny* is when you fight against the leaders of a group. The mutineers were from a ship called the *Bounty. Mutiny on the Bounty* is a famous movie.

In 2004, only 46 people lived on Pitcairn Island. The island is a dependency of Great Britain. This means that it is under the care of Great Britain.

Find Pitcairn Island on the map above. Think about living on such a small island. Think about how difficult it is to get to and what life would be like with so few people around. Decide if you would like to live on Pitcairn Island. Write four reasons why or why not.

_____

_____

_____

_____

Name _____ **Date** _____

Activity 13

One country has been born twice. How can this be? In 1947, the British passed an act called the India Independence Act. This act made India an independent country. At the same time, it made Pakistan a separate nation. East Pakistan did not feel that the new leaders were taking care of them, especially since most of the new leaders came from West Pakistan. For example, Urdu became the national language, yet in East Pakistan most of the people spoke Bengali.

A **civil** war started in 1971. A civil war is a fight within a country between the people of that country. In 1972, East Pakistan became an independent country again. It became Bangladesh.

Bangladesh was born twice because first it gained

    A. independence from Urdu and then from Bengali

    B. independence from Bengali and then from Urdu

    C. independence from Britain and then from Pakistan

    D. independence from Pakistan and then from Britain

On the map below, find and label India, Pakistan, and Bangladesh.

Which Hemispheres are they in? (Pick two.)

    A. Northern

    B. Southern

    C. Eastern

    D. Western

Which ocean, bay, and sea are they next to? _____

_____

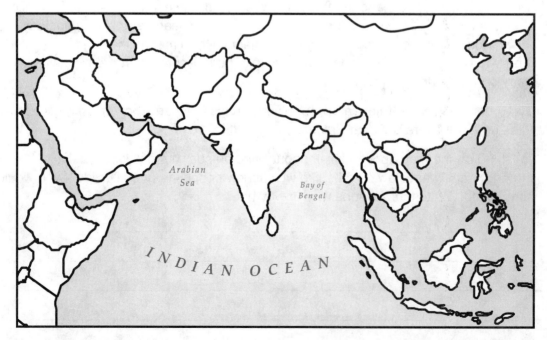

How People Shape Earth's Surface

What I Need to Know

Vocabulary

- lithosphere
- hydrosphere
- biosphere
- atmosphere
- environment
- levee
- reservoir
- lock
- terrace

About How People Shape Earth's Surface

Earth can be divided into four parts. The parts are air, water, land, and living things. All the parts are linked together. Sometimes, a change in one part may lead to changes in other parts. Some changes are natural, while others are man-made. The change may mean that people have to find a new way of living and doing things.

What I Do

Complete the Activities. When you are done, you will know about two big man-made shortcuts, why butterflies are important, and an animal in the United States that almost went extinct.

Name _____ **Date** _____

Activity 1

Geography is the study of Earth. Earth has been divided into the following four spheres:

The **lithosphere** is rock or land.

The **hydrosphere** is water.

The **biosphere** is life.

The **atmosphere** is air.

Fill in the chart by putting the words where they belong. Add one item of your own to each sphere.

Sphere	Things in this sphere

> mountain   rainforest   oxygen   sand   strait   butte   animals   insects
>
> dust in the air   smoke   ice   sea   people   canyon   marsh   air pollution

Activity 2

Our **environment** is made of everything around us. People's actions can shape the environment. For example, people can build a dam, which can stop a river from flooding. People can use the water from the dam to make electricity to light their homes and to irrigate crops.

One change leads to other changes. The dam may mean more houses are built because there is more power. The dam may also mean that more land crops are raised because there is a way to water them. This means that more land is cleared for the houses and farmland.

Which is not an example of how people can shape the environment?

  A. They can cut down trees to build a parking lot.

  B. They can plow under prairie grasses to plant wheat.

  C. They can study how Emperor penguins walk to their nests away from the ocean.

  D. They can build a **levee**, a bank or wall, to keep a river from overflowing.

Describe a recent change in your environment. It may be a new road, shopping area, or housing area.

_____

_____

Name _____ **Date** _____

Activity 3

People in Florida changed the environment. They cleared large areas and drained many wetlands, which had an effect on plant and animal life. The American alligator was one animal that was greatly affected. Forty years ago, American alligators were almost extinct. When something is extinct, its kind is no longer living and has died out.

What would not explain the American alligator almost becoming extinct?

A. over hunting

B. the draining of wetlands

C. clearing large areas of land

D. turning land into a nature preserve

What does the word *extinct* mean?

_____

_____

Find Florida on the map. Which state north of Florida borders the Atlantic Ocean?

_____

Which direction is Florida from where you live? _____

Activity 4

Every year alligators are counted in Florida. They are counted at night. Scientists go out on a boat, shine a bright light, and count the red eyes glowing on the water surface. They estimate an alligator's age by its size. Scientists go to about 50 locations, and the entire count takes about a month.

In 2006, scientists found 754 alligators in just one small section of Lake Okeechobee. The scientists looked at all their data and estimated that there are more than one million alligators in Florida. This is an amazing number, especially since alligators were almost extinct! The scientists will use this estimate to determine how many hunting permits they will hand out.

Write the numeral for one million. _____

Find and label Lake Okeechobee on the map above.

What is Florida's capital? _____. Label it on the map.

The capital is which direction from Lake Okeechobee?

A. SW   **C.** NW

B. SE   **D.** NE

Name _____ **Date** _____

Activity 5

Fill in the correct sphere.

The water you drink and use to bathe is part of the _____ .

The air you breathe and that plants take in is part of the _____ .

The food you eat comes from the _____ .

You grow your food and live on the _____ .

Many people in the Maldives drink rainwater. Big **reservoirs**, which are places where water is stored, are built on top of schools and other buildings.

On the map, find and label the Maldives.

Does your water comes from a well, rain, or a reservoir? _____

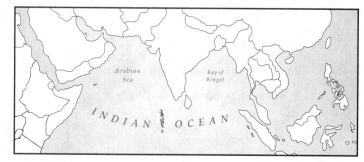

Many people do not have running water and spend a large part of each day carrying water to their homes. Would you have time to go to school if you had to spend a large part of each day carrying water to your home? Why or why not? _____

Activity 6

Think about the alligator population in Florida. The population was down 40 years ago. Today, it is up.

Now, think about your own community. List at least 10 different animals or plants that used to live in or presently live in your area. Some of the animals or plants may be extinct. Others may be newly introduced. Then estimate how many animals or plants will live in your area in the future.

		Animals		Plants	
		Type	Number	Type	Number
Future	100 years from now				
	50 years from now				
Present	Today				
Past	50 years ago				
	100 years ago				

Name _____ **Date** _____

Activity 7

Butterflies play an important role in nature. They carry pollen from plant to plant as they fly from flower to flower. This helps plants make new seeds. In turn, the new seeds make new plants.

Many kinds of butterflies live in tropical rainforests. In Taiwan, people sell butterflies. They export 15 million butterflies a year, and sell them to butterfly collectors.

Butterflies are exported, but the population of butterflies in Taiwan does not go down. One reason may be that most of the butterflies are collected:

A. from the wild

B. during the night

C. from areas near the city

D. after their eggs have been laid

Find Taiwan on the map. Which strait separates Taiwan from Mainland China?

_____

Does the Tropic of Cancer or Capricorn run through Taiwan? _____

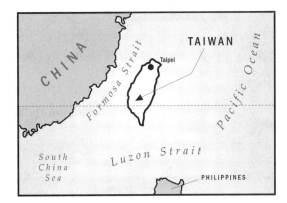

Activity 8

We do not know all the different kinds of butterflies that exist because we still do not know a lot about rainforests. We have yet to explore all of them. We do know that there are more than 10,000 different kinds of butterflies in the tropical rainforests of South and Central America alone!

Clearing rainforests is not good for butterflies. We are losing butterflies we do not even know about yet. Losing butterflies is not good for many animals, as well as plants, because butterflies are near the bottom of the food chain. Birds, especially, eat many butterflies. This is because birds can catch butterflies both in the air and on the ground.

From the story, you can tell that rainforests are an

A. important part of the biosphere

B. important part of the atmosphere

C. important part of the hydrosphere

D. important part of the lithosphere

Name a country in South and Central America that has tropical rainforests.

_____

About how many different kinds of butterflies have you seen where you live? _____

Name _____ **Date** _____

Activity 9

People helped shape the world with two big shortcuts. One of the shortcuts is the Suez Canal in Egypt, which cuts through Asia and Africa. It is 100 miles (161 km) long, which makes it the longest canal in the world that does not require locks. A **lock** is a section of a canal that can be closed off by gates. When a lock is closed off, water levels can be raised or lowered. Locks are not needed in the Suez Canal because the water levels of the Mediterranean Sea and the Gulf of Suez are about the same.

Many trade goods are shipped through the Suez Canal. For example, a lot of oil from the Middle East going to Europe or North America goes through the Suez Canal. This saves the oil from having to travel all the way around:

A. Asia

C. South America

B. Africa

D. North America

Find the Suez Canal on the map.

Which two seas does the Suez Canal connect?

_____

_____

Activity 10

An *isthmus* is a narrow strip of land that is bordered on two sides by water and land masses. The country of Panama has an isthmus through which a very important canal was dug. It was a big project on which over 80,000 people worked. About 20,000 of those workers died from accidents and disease.

The Panama Canal opened in 1914. The canal is about 51 miles (82 km) long and consists of a series of locks. The canal was very important because it was a big shortcut that saved a lot of time. For example, a ship sailing from New York City to San Francisco did not have to go around South America any longer. It could sail right through the canal. The shortcut shortened the trip by about

A. 80 miles (128.7 km)

B. 800 miles (1,287 km)

C. 8,000 miles (12,870 km)

D. 80,000 miles (128,700 km)

What is an isthmus? _____

_____

On the map, find Panama and label the Panama Canal.

Name _____ Date _____

Activity 11

In Egypt, there are 100,000 acres (405 sq. km) of land that were once desert. The desert land was changed into farmland when a dam was built. The dam is 364 feet (111 m) tall and 12,565 feet (4 km) long.

The Aswan Dam is on the Nile River by Lake Nasser. It was completed in 1970 and is used for three things: to control flooding on the Nile; to generate, or make, electricity; and to provide water for crop irrigation.

How did the dam transform desert into farmland?

A. It controlled flooding on the Nile River.

B. It generated, or made, electricity.

C. It provided water for crop irrigation.

On the map, find Egypt, Lake Nasser, and the city of Aswan. (The Aswan Dam is near Aswan.)

Which direction are the Red Sea and the Mediterranean Sea from Aswan? _____

Are there any dams near you? If so, name them. _____

Activity 12

In the Philippines, giant staircases were made that cover an area of 4,000 square miles (10,360 sq km) and go 6,000 feet (2 km) up a mountainside. The staircases are **terraces**, which are flat platforms of earth cut or built into mountainsides. Terraces make it so more land is usable and help to slow erosion.

The giant terraces were built over 2,000 years—ago and they are still used today! They are used to grow rice, which is one of the most important food crops in the world. The other most important food crops are wheat, corn, and potatoes.

Look at the two pictures on the right. Which picture shows the most usable land? Why? _____

_____

Can you identify below what the four most important food crops look like as they are growing?

_____   _____   _____   _____

Name _____

Date _____

Activity 13

Tarsiers are tiny mammals that live in the Philippines. Their bodies are 3.5 to 6 inches (9–15 cm) long. They have large eyes and tails twice as long as their bodies. Also, they have very long digits. (On animals, digits are like fingers and toes; they are not numbers!)

Tarsiers are nocturnal, which means they sleep during the day and are awake at night. Their big, round digit tips help them cling vertically to trees and catch themselves as they leap from trunk to trunk. Tarsiers eat insects and have been known to eat birds.

Find the Philippines on the map.

Use the location of the Philippines and the behavior of the tarsiers to help you answer the question.

Tarsiers will most likely not be able to survive in the wild if we

- **A.** plow under grasslands to turn it into farmland

- **B.** build dams to change desert land into farmland

- **C.** cut down temperate forests to clear land for farming

- **D.** cut down tropical rainforests to clear land for farming

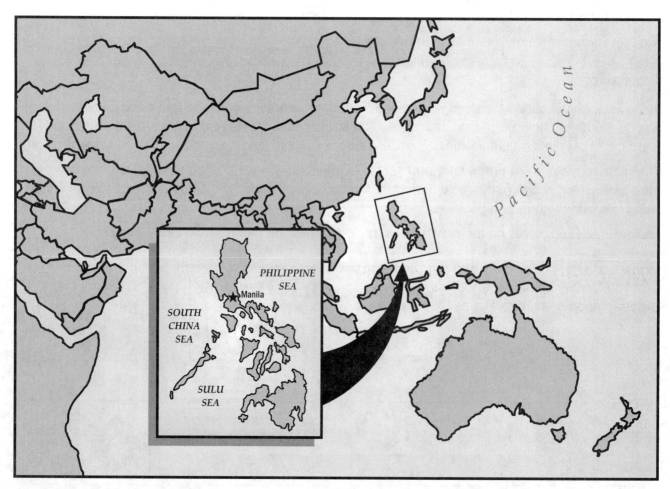

How Earth's Surface Shapes How People Live

What I Need to Know

Vocabulary

- monsoon
- adapt
- salt pan
- hazard
- traditional
- treaty

About How Earth's Surface Shapes How People Live

Earth's surface shapes what we do and how we adapt to what is around us. For example, we might build a house on stilts in an area where it rains a lot. We might sail at certain times of the year because we know the direction the winds will be blowing. We might invent something new to be used in a particular place, and we usually adapt our clothes to fit the climate we live in.

What I Do

Complete the Activities. When you are done, you will know about a hotel made of salt, what was invented so that people could practice ice hockey in the summer, and what made the loudest sound ever heard on Earth.

Name _____   **Date** _____

Activity 1

Winters are very cold in Minnesota, but this does not keep people from being outdoors. They ice fish, cross-country ski, snowboard, and play hockey. Two students wanted to practice hockey even in the warm summer. So, they invented something to be able to do it: they took the blades off their ice skates and replaced them with wheels. They invented in-line skates!

From the story, you can tell that

   A. where we live can affect what we do

   B. people who play hockey do not ice fish

   C. all inventors in Minnesota are students

   D. in-line skates cannot be used in the winter

Find Minnesota on the map. Which Great Lake borders Minnesota? _____

Which country borders Minnesota, and in what direction? _____

About how many hundreds of miles is it from where you live to Minnesota? _____

What river, which flows all the way to the Gulf of Mexico, starts in Minnesota?

_____

Activity 2

In Cambodia, many of the houses are built on stilts. Houses built off the ground most likely mean that

   A. Cambodia is a very dry country   **B.** Cambodia is a very wet country

Cambodia has a monsoonal climate. **Monsoons** are heavy winds that change direction twice a year. From November to April, days in Cambodia are sunny, clear, and dry. This is because the monsoon winds blow across the land to the ocean.

From May to October, it rains every day in Cambodia. This is because the monsoon winds change direction. They blow across the ocean to the land. The winds pick up water from the ocean and drop it on the land. By the end of the rainy season, it is not uncommon for many of the roads and rice fields to be covered with a foot (30 cm) of water.

Find Cambodia on the map. Which countries are to the north and west of it?

_____

_____

What country most likely has a monsoonal climate?

   A. India

   B. Chad

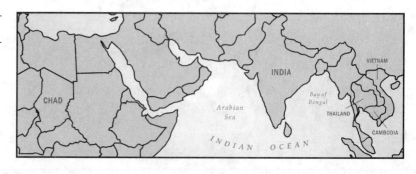

Name _____ **Date** _____

Activity 3

When people **adapt**, they adjust or change, to be able to fit. Sometimes people must adapt to fit their physical environments. Think about where you live and your physical environment. What are the summers like? What are the winters like? Are there mountains or lakes? List how you have adapted the following things to your physical environment.

Clothing:_____

_____

House styles:_____

_____

Recreation (fun things to do): _____

_____

Food: _____

Agriculture (what crops you grow): _____

_____

Jobs: _____

_____

Activity 4

Native Americans lived all across North America. Different groups had different cultures, and each group adapted to its environment.

Igloos are domed houses. They are made from blocks of frozen snow. They are not permanent houses, they are temporary houses. Most likely they are used during the

   A. fishing season of the Pacific Northwest region

   B. seal-hunting season in the central Arctic region

   C. buffalo-hunting season of the Great Plains region

Teepees were made of buffalo skins and wooden poles. Why do you think teepees were very good homes for Native Americans who followed the buffalo across the central Plains?

   A. They could be easily moved.

   B. They could be built on top of each other.

   C. They could be raised on stilts when it rained.

On another sheet of paper, describe or draw a picture of what Native American homes in your area looked like. On the lines below, list two ways the homes were adapted to the environment.

_____

_____

Name _____ **Date** _____

Activity 5

In Bolivia, the building material of one hotel was adapted to fit its environment. It is made entirely of salt! The walls, floors, chairs, tables, and even the beds in the hotel are all made of salt. Chainsaws are used to cut it into blocks.

The hotel is in a **salt pan**, which is where salt has been left on the floor of a desert basin. A basin is like a wide, shallow bowl. The salt pan is called the Salar de Uyuni salt pan, and it is estimated that it contains more than 10 billion tons (10.2 billion metric tons) of salt!

Bolivia is landlocked, which means that Bolivia has

A. a sea or ocean coastline

B. no sea or ocean coastline

List all of Bolivia's neighbors. _____

_____

_____

Does Bolivia have more or fewer neighbors than your country?

_____

Are any of your neighbors the same as Bolivia's?

_____

Activity 6

A **hazard** is a danger. A natural hazard is not man-made; it happens in and is caused by nature. A natural hazard may be a flood, a windstorm, a tornado, or an earthquake.

Think about where you live. List some natural hazards. _____

_____

Are these hazards different or the same as hazards in other parts of your region?

_____

How has your community or region adapted to these hazards (where houses are built, alarm systems, emergency services, etc.)?

_____

_____

_____

_____

_____

Name _____ **Date** _____

Activity 7

A **tradition** is a custom or belief handed down over time. A tradition represents something has always been done in a certain way over time. Some traditional homes in south central China were all built with gables, which are the end walls of a building. The gables were made with baked clay bricks. The baked bricks were covered in plaster and were then topped with clay tiles. These traditional homes had gables built onto the roofs because of a hazard.

From which hazard would you guess that gables most likely protect a house?

   A. fire   **B.** flood   **C.** tornado   **D.** earthquake

The gables were built as fire barriers. Traditional houses were built close together. The gables helped stop fire from spreading.

Find south central China on the map.

Which is closer to south central China: Laos or Mongolia? _____

China is in which two hemispheres? _____

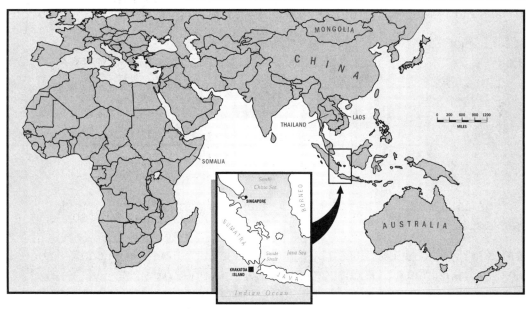

Activity 8

A natural hazard led to the loudest sound in recorded history. Which would you guess was the natural hazard?

   A. a tornado   **B.** a volcano   **C.** a hurricane   **D.** an earthquake

In 1883, the largest volcanic eruption in modern history took place. It was on the island of Krakatau in Indonesia. Krakatau is in the center of the Sunda Strait, which is between the islands of Java and Sumatra. The sound of the volcanic eruption was heard nearly 3,000 miles (4,828 km) away!

On the map, find the places mentioned above. Draw a circle with its center in the Sunda Strait and a radius of about 3,000 miles.

Could you have heard the explosion if you were in Australia, Thailand, or Somalia? _____

Name _____ **Date** _____

Activity 9

When Mt. Vesuvius erupted in Italy in 79 CE, people breathed in poisonous volcanic gases. They were buried in ash and rock. More than 16,000 people died in the cities of Pompeii and Herculaneum.

In 1749, the city of Pompeii was dug out. Artifacts and people were almost perfectly preserved. (An artifact is a thing made by human work or skill.) This made it easier for researchers to learn about life in the city of long ago. Today, you can walk among the parts of a city that have been uncovered. The ancient city is just a little southeast of Naples.

On the map, find Italy and the city of Naples. Italy looks like a high-heeled boot kicking a rock. The "rock" is part of Italy. What is the island called? _____

Which three seas surround Italy?

A. Adriatic, Black, Caspian

B. Mediterranean, Red, Ionic

C. Mediterranean, Black, Ionic

D. Ionian, Tyrrhenian, Adriatic

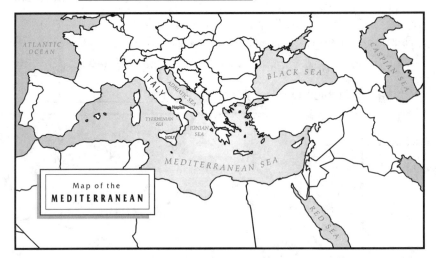

Map of the
MEDITERRANEAN

Activity 10

A **treaty** is an agreement between two nations. Treaties deal with peace and/or trade. They may also have to do with pollution.

Think about acid rain. Acid rain is caused by fumes (gases and smoke) from cars, factories, and power stations. In the air, the fumes change into acids, and winds blow the acids away. Far away, rain falls. The rain is acid because of fumes let into the air from far away! Acid rain harms trees, crops, and fish.

Trees in southeastern Canada were dying from acid rain. Part of the problem may have been pollution from factories in the

A. southeastern United States blowing east

B. southwestern United States blowing east

C. northeastern United States blowing north

D. northwestern United States blowing north

What is a treaty? _____

Name _____ **Date** _____

Activity 11

Which natural hazard would you guess could cause a "year without summer"?

A. a tornado   **C.** a hurricane

B. a volcano   **D.** an earthquake

In the eastern United States and Canada, the months of June, July, and August are usually hot summer months. But one year, there was no summer. There was even some snow and frost.

This was due to the volcanic eruption of Mount Tambora in Indonesia in 1815. The blast was so enormous that the ash shot into the air and blocked sunlight. The ash cloud was carried on air currents, and it blocked sunlight as far away as the eastern United States and Canada.

From the story, you can tell that

A. air currents do not affect climate

B. natural events have no affect on the climate

C. what happens in one country may affect the climate of another country

D. the amount of sunlight reaching Earth cannot be changed

On the map, find and mark a state in the eastern United States and a province in eastern Canada.

Activity 12

What is the population of Antarctica? Zero! Some scientists live there for short amounts of time, but they do not live there all the time. There are no permanent cities or towns in Antarctica. One big reason is the climate. The lowest temperature on Earth was recorded in 1983 in Antarctica. It was −128.6°F (−89°C). If you spit when it is this cold, your spit freezes before it even hits the ground! Of course, Antarctica can warm up. In the summer it heats up to 0°F (−18°C).

One reason Antarctica is colder than the Arctic is because it has a higher elevation. The Arctic is at sea level. Antarctica has an average elevation of about 6,500 feet (2 km).

What is the population of your city and state? _____

What are usual winter and summer temperatures? _____

How does climate affect your city and state populations? _____

How do landforms, elevation, and the location of your city and state affect the climate?

_____

Name _____ **Date** _____

Activity 13

Armidale is a city in Australia in New South Wales that has a high elevation. School children in Armidale wear uniforms, including hats. The hats have wide brims, and the children must wear them at recess. During recess, children who forgot their hats at home must stay in the shade. Wearing hats is a way people have adapted to where they live.

Australian school children probably wear wide-brimmed hats to protect them from

  A. running too fast

  B. burning their eyes

  C. the cold when it is cloudy

  D. skin damage caused by the sun

Look at a reference map of Australia. Then, from memory, sketch a map of Australia in the box below. Draw the borders and write the names of these states and territories:

Western Australia	New South Wales
Queensland	South Australia
Tasmania	Victoria
Australian Capital Territory	Northern Territory

On your map, mark where Armidale is.

Resources from Earth

What I Need to Know

About Resources from Earth

Different countries on Earth have different resources. Some countries or places are rich in resources, while others have very few. We use or want different resources at different times, and we trade them and transport them from country to country. There is a limited supply of some resources, which means that we can run out if we are not careful.

Vocabulary

- renewable

- limited

- flow

What I Do

Complete the exercises in the Daily Warm-Ups. When you are done, you will know what Iceland and Idaho have in common, what country's name means "silver," and what the nickname "Tar Heel State" means. You will also know about some natural resources that are traded.

Name _____ **Date** _____

Activity 1

A resource is a supply of something that takes care of a need. A natural resource is found in nature; it is not man-made. Some resources are **renewable**, which means that we can grow or get more of them. Some resources are not renewable, meaning there is a **limited** supply—in other words once it is used up, it is gone. Other resources **flow**. We use the flow or movement of the resource to take care of our needs.

Below is a list of natural resources. Place each resource under the correct heading.

wind copper oil plants timber

oxygen water fish coal minerals

Renewable	Nonrenewable	Flow
1.	1.	1.
2.	2.	2.
3.	3.	
4.	4.	

Write one sentence to describe how you use each type of natural resource: renewable, nonrenewable, and flow.

1. _____

2. _____

3. _____

Activity 2

North Carolina's nickname comes from a natural resource. Its nickname is the "Tar Heel State." Its natural resource is tar. When North Carolina was still a colony, its tar was used on English ships.

Think about tar. It is sticky. During the Civil War, soldiers from North Carolina refused to retreat. When one retreats, one turns and goes back. The soldiers stuck to their ground, as if their heels were glued to the ground with tar. Soldiers from North Carolina said they would put tar on the heels of those who had retreated so that the soldiers would "stick better in the next fight."

Today, people come to North Carolina to see its beautiful beaches and mountains. Farmers there grow crops such as tobacco, cotton, and soybeans. The natural beauty and good soil of North Carolina are like tar in that they are _____.

Find North Carolina on the map. Which states and ocean border North Carolina?

Name _____ **Date** _____

Activity 3

North Carolina has two industries that depend on its forest resources. Circle them below.

A. banking   **C.** textile mills

B. paper mills   **D.** furniture making

If North Carolina wants to continue these industries, it must

   A. start to use more plastic

   B. find a cheaper way to cut down trees

   C. clear all the land so it can plant new forests

   D. plant new trees at the same rate it is using old ones

Name a renewable, nonrenewable, and flow resource from your state.

renewable: _____

nonrenewable: _____

flow: _____

Have some industries in your state died out because resources were used up? Explain your answer.

_____

_____

Activity 4

Argentina is known for its beef, and many cattle are raised there. Argentina's name gives you a hint about another one of its natural resources. *Argentum* is the Latin word for "silver," and *argentino* is the Spanish word for "silvery." Early explorers returned to Spain with pieces of silver from the country known today as Argentina, which started a silver rush in the country.

Today, silver is mined in more than 60 countries. Alaska and Nevada produce more than 70 percent of the silver mined in the United States.

Color in seven parts of the circle to show how much of the total of U.S. silver is mined in Alaska and Nevada.

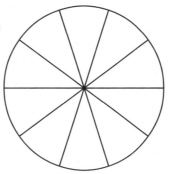

On the map, find Alaska, Nevada, and Argentina. Are they all on the same continent? _____

Is Nevada closer to Alaska or Argentina?_____

Name _____ **Date** _____

Activity 5

Countries trade their natural resources with other countries because not everyone has the same natural resources. Some countries have more natural resources than others.

Copper is a mineral used in building construction and in electrical products. Using the information below, label the countries on the map where most of the copper is mined. For the United States, label the states that are listed.

1. Chile	**2.** United States (Arizona, New Mexico, Utah)	**3.** Indonesia
4. Peru	**5.** Australia **6.** Russia **7.** China	**8.** Canada

Is copper found in every hemisphere? _____

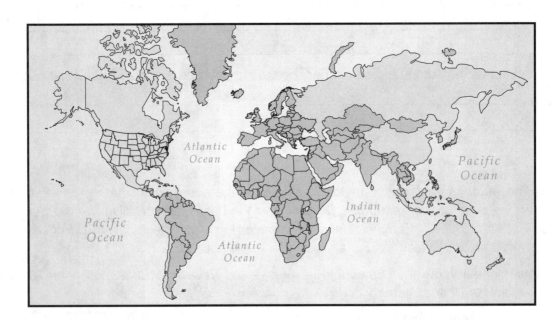

Activity 6

Zinc is a mineral that is often used as a protective coating on steel. It is also used in rubber and paints. Using the information below, label the countries on the map that are leading producers of zinc. For the United States, label the states that are listed.

1. China	**2.** Australia	**3.** Peru	**4.** Canada
5. United States (Alaska, Missouri, Tennessee)			**6.** Mexico

Write which direction these countries are from the United States. _____

_____

Now, write which direction these countries are from Australia. _____

_____

Name _____ **Date** _____

Activity 7

Many people in El Salvador cook using firewood. As soon as they are done cooking, they remove the burning sticks of wood from the fire, put out the flames, and bang the wood against the floor to make sure there are no lit sparks.

These actions tell you what is most likely true about El Salvador?

A. There is plenty of firewood.   **C.** People do not like their food cooked a lot.

B. Firewood is hard to get.   **D.** People know food is ready when they hear banging.

Many people in El Salvador are poor. A civil war took place in El Salvador from 1980 to 1992 and people are still recovering from it. By putting out the fire, people can reuse the firewood. They can cook one or two more meals with it, and this saves time and money.

Find El Salvador on the map. What makes this country different from all the other countries in Central America? (Hint: Atlantic Ocean) _____

Activity 8

One of El Salvador's first major exports was an indigo dye. Indigo is a deep violet-blue color. The dye came from the leaves of a native plant, one of El Salvador's natural resources. Then, in the early 1800s, the market for indigo fell and it was no longer a major export. However, people still liked the color.

One likely reason indigo dye was no longer a major export is

A. cheaper man-made dyes were invented   **C.** all the plant leaves were burned to cook food

B. no one liked the color indigo anymore   **D.** people who wore the color indigo got in trouble

What countries border El Salvador and in what direction? _____

Is El Salvador in the tropics? Explain why or why not. _____

Name _____ **Date** _____

Activity 9

Nonrenewable resources can be used up. When they are gone, there are no more. Many of the resources we use for energy are nonrenewable, such as natural gas and oil. Presently, the United States is using its own natural gas and oil, but it is also buying oil from other countries. Many people fear this is making us too dependent on other countries. On the map, color the countries listed below where the United States buys oil.

Mexico	Iraq	Canada	Angola	Saudi Arabia
Venezuela	Russia	Nigeria	United Kingdom	Ecuador

Most likely, this oil is transported from the country to the United States by

A. train   **B.** railroad   **C.** river badger   **D.** ocean tanker

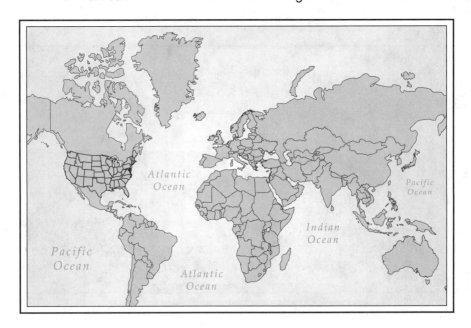

Activity 10

What could Iceland and the state of Idaho have in common? They both have a natural resource called geothermal energy. Below the surface of the Earth there is hot magma, which is liquid rock. The magma heats water and the hot water is used to heat buildings. In Iceland, over 86 percent of all households are heated with geothermal energy. In Idaho, the capitol building in Boise is heated with geothermal energy.

Which is not true about geothermal energy?

A. It comes from hot magma.   **C.** It can be used to heat households.

B. It is a natural resource.   **D.** It is only used in the Southern Hemisphere.

On the map, find Iceland and Idaho, and label each capital.

Which place is closer to the Arctic Circle? _____

Name _____ **Date** _____

Activity 11

The United States buys oil from other countries, but it also produces its own oil. Using the information below, mark the top ten oil-producing states on the map by writing the number inside the state.

1. Texas	2. Alaska	3. California	4. Louisiana
5. New Mexico	6. Oklahoma	7. Wyoming	8. Kansas
9. North Dakota	10. Montana		

Offshore drilling is oil drilling that takes place in the ocean. Which four states listed above probably include offshore drilling?

_____

_____

_____

How do you heat and cool your home? Where does the energy source come from?

_____

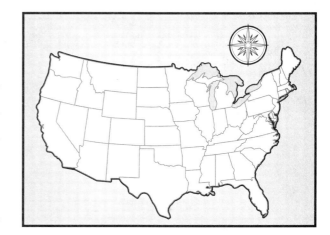

Activity 12

Resources like oil can be used up, because they are nonrenewable. For this reason, people want to find different ways of getting energy. Wind is a different source of energy and windmills can be used to produce that type of energy. Some countries such as Denmark and Britain have started wind farms in the North and Baltic Seas.

There is talk of setting up wind farms in the Great Lakes of the United States. Winds over water are usually stronger and more consistent, and off-shore windmills can make about two times the amount of energy as windmills on a shore. But some people do not want the wind farms. They say the windmills will ruin the view and hurt tourism and fishing.

Are you for or against wind farms in the Great Lakes? Why?_____

_____

_____

On the map, find and label Denmark, Britain, the North and Baltic Seas, and the Great Lakes.

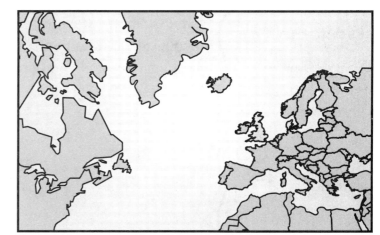

Understanding the Past

About Understanding the Past

Places change over time. The changes may be in animal and plant populations, or people can change places by building things such as dams or roads. We can chart changes in population in graphs, and we can look at maps from the past and the present to see how cities have grown. We can also talk to people to find out how their views about places have changed.

What I Need to Know

Vocabulary

- scurvy

What I Do

Complete the Activities. When you are done, you will know about a man who was traveling for so long that his relatives did not recognize him when he got back. You will know about the first American in space, and about a time when locusts were so thick that they covered the ground.

Name _____ **Date** _____

Activity 1

Make three quick sketches of dwellings (homes). They should look like dwellings built where you live. One should be from long ago, of the type a Native American would live in; one dwelling should look like what some of the first settlers lived in; and one should be what dwellings look like today.

Why is the dwelling you drew for today bigger than the ones from long ago?

_____

_____

Would you expect the people who lived in these dwellings to all have the same jobs?

_____

_____

Activity 2

Think of a place that has a historical name. It can be a place near where you live, your state, a faraway city, or your school.

For example, there is a school in Indiana called William Henry Harrison High School. The school was named after the man who was president in 1841. He was only president for one month when he got ill and passed away. He served the shortest term of any U.S. president.

This high school is in Lafayette, a city named after the Marquis de Lafayette. Lafayette was French, but he served as a major general under George Washington.

Write four sentences about the name of the place you chose._____

_____

_____

On the map, find and label Lafayette, Indiana, and the place you wrote about.

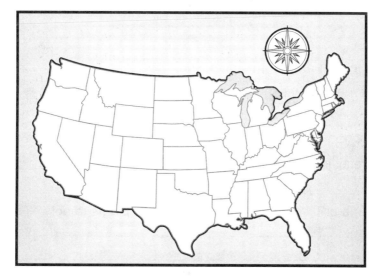

Name _____ **Date** _____

Activity 3

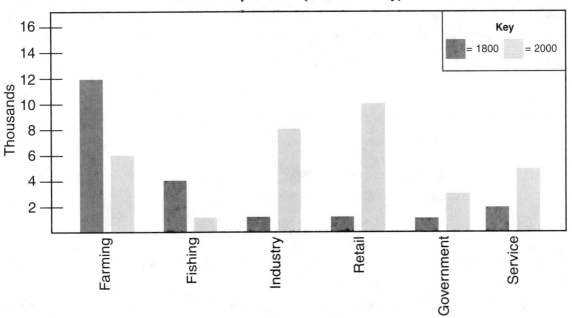

Where People Work (Track County)

Industry jobs are any jobs in a business that makes something. Retail jobs are in stores or where things are sold. Government jobs are where people work in places run by the government, such as the post office, parks, or courts. Service jobs involve doing things like serving food or cleaning.

What might be a likely government job in 1800 in Track County?

A. hat maker   **C.** wheat farrner

B. blacksmith   **D.** schoolteacher

Less people farm in 2000 than did in 1800, but today's farms produce more food. Why do you think this is so?

A. There are more stores.   **C.** People started to eat fish.

B. There are better equipment and seeds.   **D.** People left the farm to work in factories.

Activity 4

Use the graph from Activity 3 to answer the questions.

What might explain the large increase in industry jobs?

A. a high school   **C.** a county courthouse

B. an amusement park   **D.** a computer-assembly plant

Why would service and retail jobs go up when industry jobs go up? _____

_____

Would you expect the same or different types of animals and plants to do well in Track County in 1800 and 2000? Why? _____

_____

Name _____ **Date** _____

Activity 5

Think about your community and a person who has changed it. The person may or may not be living, and he or she may have helped the community by:

- making a park
- starting recycling efforts
- donating land for a school
- opening a store
- clearing land and building houses
- starting a manufacturing plant that gave many people jobs

Write three sentences about how the person changed the community. _____

_____

Do you like the changes? Why or why not? _____

_____

Activity 6

June 7, 1870

Dear Abigail,

I am not going to school anymore. It is two miles away. There are so many locusts that I cannot stand to walk barefoot. I need to save my shoes for the winter. All the crops have been eaten. All the grass has been eaten. There is nothing on the ground but locusts. The locusts came in a big cloud. They blocked out the sun.

Your friend,

Sarah

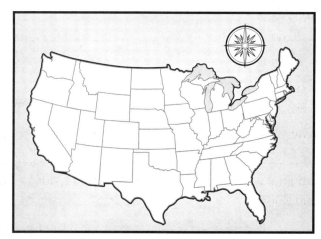

This letter tells us about a time in the 1870s when locusts destroyed many prairie farms in Canada and the United States. The kind of locusts that destroyed the farms have died out, but there are different locusts in Africa that still destroy farms today.

On another sheet of paper, write a letter to a friend. In your letter, give a reason why you might not go to school for a while. Think about how different your reason is from Sarah's.

Which states are prairie states?

A. Iowa, Kansas, Nebraska

B. Texas, Florida, Alabama

C. Maine, Missouri, California

D. Oklahoma, Oregon, South Dakota

Name _____   **Date** _____

Activity 7

Old buildings can teach us about people long ago. For example, many old castles have round towers at the corners. Imagine you are standing inside at the top of a tower going downstairs. Would you guess that the stairs go down clockwise or counterclockwise?

A. clockwise

B. counter clockwise

Long ago, people were taught to fight with swords. People held the swords in their right hands. People defending the tower would be at the top of the stairs. They would want their right hands free to swing. They would not want their sword arms to hit the wall. For that reason, the stairs, from the top of the tower down, go counterclockwise. What does this mean for the attackers?

A. The wall would not be in the way of their sword arms.

B. The wall would stop their sword arms from swinging full force.

Many stone castles with round towers for defense were built in Ireland, England, and Germany. Find these countries on the map. Which of these countries is closest to the prime meridian?

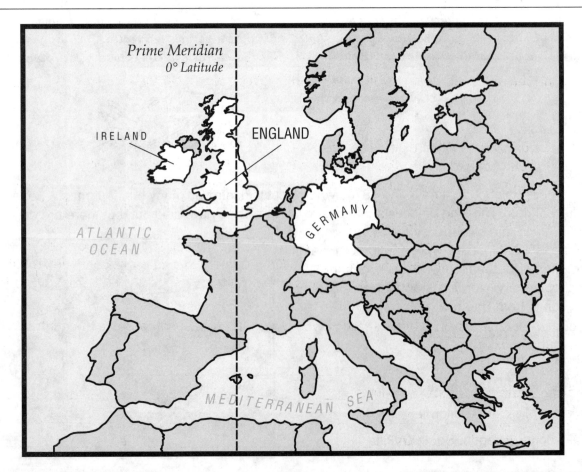

Name _____ **Date** _____

Activity 8

Marco Polo was born around 1254 in Venice. He was a merchant and a traveler. He traveled for so long that when he returned home, his family didn't recognize him. On the map, trace the route of Marco Polo using a colored pencil:

1. Start in Venice, Italy.

2. Go to Acre, a port city, and then Jerusalem (both are cities in Israel today).

3. Travel through what are now Turkey, Iraq, and Iran to the port of Hormuz on the Persian Gulf.

4. Travel north and east through Afghanistan, across the Gobi Desert in China, to what is today Beijing.

5. Sail south through the South China Sea, stopping in Vietnam, Malaysia, and Sumatra.

6. Stop in Sri Lanka and then go up along the west coast of India, finally returning back to Venice after 24 years.

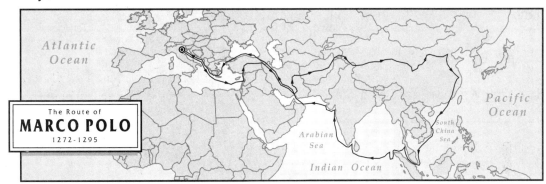

Do you think you could recognize someone if you did not see him or her for 24 years? _____

Activity 9

How did Marco Polo make his relatives realize it was him? He showed them jewels he had collected during his travels. He had hidden them by sewing them into his clothes, and brought them back to share with his family. Polo wrote a book about his travels. Many people read the book and learned about places that they did not know were real. Although Polo exaggerated, he did teach people about places that they did not know existed.

Polo told people about China and how people there burned coal for fuel. Europeans did not do that yet. He told them about paper money, which Europeans did not use at that time. He told them about a mail system that used riders on horses, the horses and riders changing constantly. With fresh riders and horses running day and night, the mail could be carried over 200 miles (362 km) in just one day.

Think of a book you have read that has taught you something about another place or country. Write the title of the book._____

What does your country use for fuel? _____

Describe your country's money system. _____

_____

How is mail carried in your country? _____

Name _____ **Date** _____

Activity 10

Alan Shepard was the first American to enter space.
Shepard was born in 1923 in East Derry, New Hampshire.
He went to school at the U.S. Naval Academy in
Annapolis, Maryland. On May 5, 1961, Shepard blasted
into space from Cape Canaveral, Florida. He went 116
miles (187 km) into space for a flight that lasted 15
minutes. His space capsule then landed in the ocean
near Bermuda. Ten years later, Shepard went into space
again and landed on the moon. He walked on its surface
in 1971.

On the map, mark where Shepard was born and where he
went to school. Mark where he blasted off into space and
where he landed. Make a key to show what each mark
means.

In which ocean is Bermuda? _____

Is Bermuda off the West or East Coast of the
United States?_____

Activity 11

Below, you are going to make a map and a chart about a time and place in history. After doing some
research, draw the map with landmarks, roads, and features such as rivers and mountains.

The chart should include information such as types of animals inhabiting the area, jobs people had,
and population.

Then write one sentence about who the people were, where they came from, or what they were like.
Write another sentence describing the physical land.

Name _____ **Date** _____

Activity 12

Several people have gone into space. Perhaps one day we will go to other planets and space travel will become common. Possibly, when people ask for our address, we will have to give them more than just our street and country address. We will have to tell them we live in a particular solar system in the Milky Way Galaxy!

Fill in the names of the planets in our solar system.

Then, write your complete address!

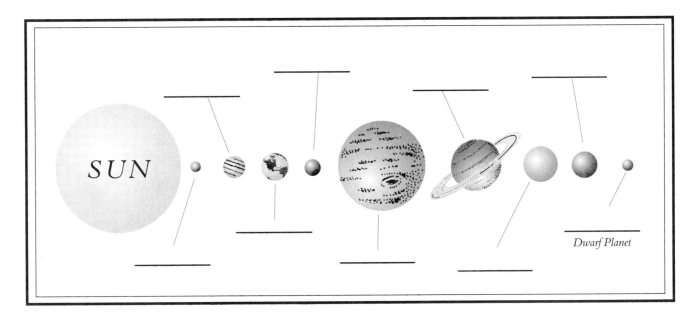

Name: _____

Street: _____

City: _____

State: _____

Country: _____

Continent: _____

Hemispheres: _____

Planet: _____

System: _____

Galaxy: _____

Name _____   **Date** _____

Activity 13

James Cook was born in 1728. He was an English explorer who led three voyages of exploration. At that time, many sailors died from **scurvy**, a disease caused from a lack of vitamin C. Cook was known for keeping his men healthy. He did not know about vitamins, but he made his men eat fresh food or pickled cabbage. He made them bathe every day and keep the ship clean.

Cook's first voyage of exploration was in 1768. Trace Cook's route on the map.

1. From England, go around South America to Tahiti.
2. Go around New Zealand to Botany Bay in Australia.
3. Go up the coast of Australia to New Guinea to Sumatra.
4. Go across the Indian Ocean up the west side of Africa and back to England.

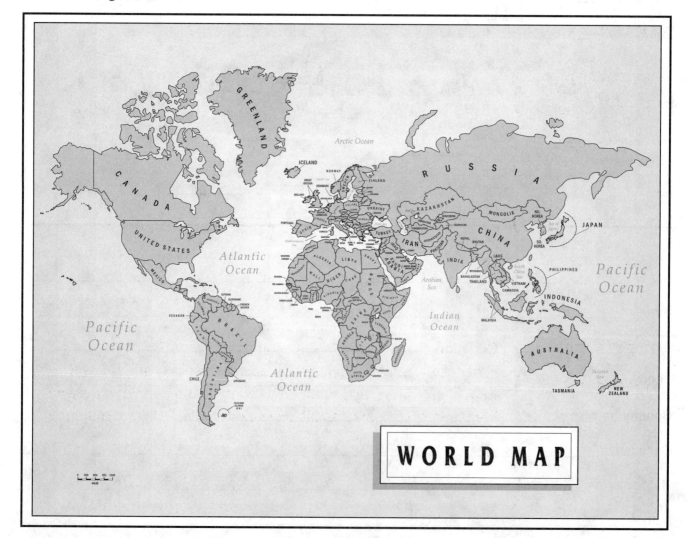

What can you eat today that helps prevent scurvy?

A. milk   **B.** sugar   **C.** oranges   **D.** crackers

Using Geography Today to Plan for the Future

What I Need to Know

Vocabulary

- life expectancy

- immunization

- conserved

What I Do

About Planning for the Future

We don't know what the future holds, but we can use geography to plan for it. We can look at past and present numbers of populations and estimate future populations. We can look at resource graphs to estimate when we will run out of resources. This will help us plan ways to save, reuse, or recycle our resources. This will also help us make a map of where we should live and why.

Complete the Activities. When you are done, you will know why Japanese warriors of long ago wrapped sharkskin around their weapons. You will also know why taking off a pump handle saved lives, and which park has the lowest point in the United States.

Name _____ **Date** _____

Activity 1

What is your life expectancy—or in other words, how long do you expect to live? Every country has a life expectancy. Of course, some people live more years than others, and some live fewer. On another sheet of paper, make a bar graph. The graph will show the average life expectancy for people in some countries.

Country	Life Expectancy
Australia	80
Austria	79
Benin	53
Bolivia	66
Central African Republic	43
Chile	77
France	80
Guatemala	69
India	64
Laos	55
Mexico	70
United States	76
Yemen	62

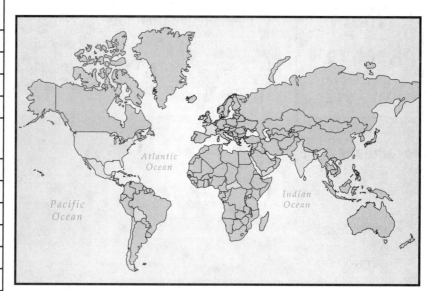

Activity 2

Use the graph you made in Activity 1.

On the map, find and label the countries from the graph.

Which two countries have the lowest life expectancy?

　　1. _____　　**2.** _____

Which continent are they are on? _____

Which two countries have the highest life expectancy?

　　1. _____　　**2.** _____

Which continents are they on?

　　1. _____　　**2.** _____

Why do some people live longer? List some things or reasons that you think help people live longer.

_____

_____

Name _____ **Date** _____

Activity 3

In 1854 in London, England, there was an outbreak of cholera, which is easily spread and can be deadly. John Snow was a doctor who tracked the disease. He saw that in just one neighborhood, over 500 people died in just 10 days. He noticed that all the people in the neighborhood shared the same well, meaning that they all got water from the same place. Dr. Snow had the handle taken off the well pump so that no one could use water from the well. All the cases of cholera stopped.

From the story, you can tell that

   A. there are no cholera outbreaks today

   B. clean water is important for one's health

   C. it is not healthy to live in neighborhoods

   D. people should not get their water from wells

On the map, find and label London, England, in Great Britain.

Activity 4

Using the information below, make a line graph that shows the world's population from past to present.

(500 million is half of a billion.)

Year	Population
1500	425 million
1600	545 million
1700	610 million
1800	900 million
1900	1.6 billion
2000	6 billion
2050	8.5 billion (estimated)

The population is most likely going up more in

   A. cities   **B.** the country

Which is not a reason for the world's population growth?

   A. More people have clean water.

   B. More people have better diets.

   C. More people have time to sleep.

   D. More people have better medical care.

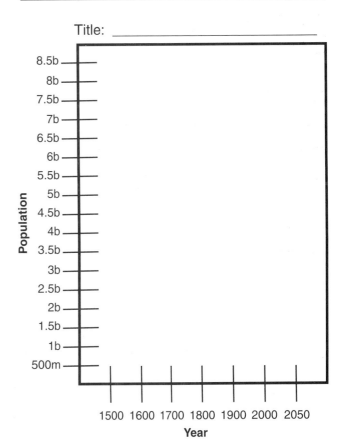

Title: _____

Name _____ **Date** _____

Activity 5

Chief Cakobau was a ruler of Fiji for many years. In 1875, he visited Australia. When he returned, he brought something back that killed one-third of his people. Cakobau did not mean to harm his people. What happened?

   A. Cakobau brought back a new weapon.

   B. Cakobau was infected with a disease.

   C. Cakobau did not bring back enough food.

   D. Cakobau did not want his people to go to Australia.

Cakobau was infected with measles. Today, we have **immunizations**. The immunizations make us immune, or protected, from a disease.

Do you think there is a connection between increased life expectancy and immunizations? Why or why not?

_____

_____

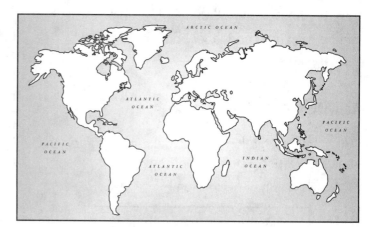

Mark where Fiji is on the map. Which ocean is it in?

_____

Which direction is it from New Zealand?

_____

Activity 6

Think about our planet's population and its resources. Having more people means using _____ resources.

   A. less   **B.** more   **C.** the same

Remember that nonrenewable resources can be used up. When they are gone, there are no more. What can we do to make sure we do not run out of these resources? We can reduce, reuse, and recycle. When we reduce, reuse, and recycle, we also make less trash.

Guess which country makes more garbage than any other country in the world. _____

Guess about how much trash in pounds is made per person per year by this country. _____

Write three ways you can reduce, reuse, and recycle so that you make less trash.

   1. _____

   2. _____

   3. _____

Name _____ **Date** _____

Activity 7

Imagine your community is starting a recycling program. It costs too much to do a house pick-up of items. You decide to have drop-off stations instead. You want the drop-off stations to be near people, and you want them to be easy to get to. Look at the map. Choose four drop-off stations. Number them on the map. Tell why you chose the places you did.

1. _____
2. _____
3. _____
4. _____

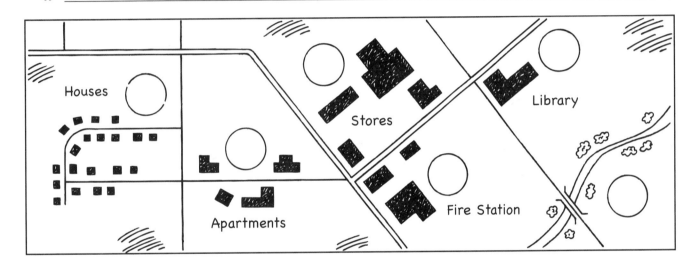

Activity 8

National parks are not city parks or state parks. They are parks owned and run by the federal government. The federal government is conserving the land. When land is **conserved**, it is kept safe from being ruined or wasted. National parks help conserve land for people, animals, and plants.

Should land be conserved? Some say national park land could be used for houses or farms. They say that trees on park land could be cut down, oil drilled, mines dug, and the land sold for money.

Others say the land should be conserved and saved for our children. We may get quick money, but we will lose more in the future, such as many species of plants and animals. We would also lose areas where we could camp, hike, swim, and go on vacation.

A national park is _____

What is the closest national park to you? _____

Give three reasons land should be conserved.

1. _____
2. _____
3. _____

Name _____　　**Date** _____

Activity 9

On the map, find and label the national parks listed below.

Glacier Bay (Alaska) has glaciers that move down the mountainside and break into the sea. It has lots of wildlife, too.

Zion (Utah) has unusual shapes and landscapes resulting from erosion. It has canyon walls up to 2,640 feet (805 m) high!

Crater Lake (Oregon) has a very blue lake. It is the deepest lake in the United States. It is in the middle of a volcanic crater. The volcano last erupted 7,700 years ago.

Death Valley (California) has the lowest point in the Western Hemisphere. It is a large desert.

The Everglades (Florida) is a swamp-filled park with the largest remaining subtropical wilderness in the continental United States.

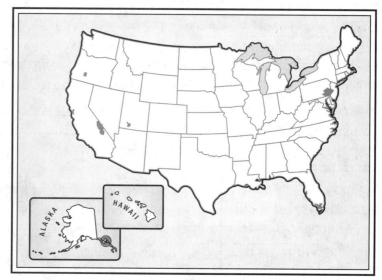

Write which direction each park is from where you live.

_____

_____

Out of the parks, which one would you most like to visit and why? _____

_____

Activity 10

Some national parks are historical national parks, not just interesting land. They are parks where key moments in history happened. One such park is the Valley Forge National Historical Park. This park is the site where George Washington and his army camped during the winter of 1777 to 1778. Washington's men had a hard time in the cold weather. Many of them did not have boots. One soldier was seen standing on his hat to keep his bare feet out of the snow.

Why might Washington have chosen to camp in Valley Forge?

　A. It made his soldiers learn how to be tough.

　B. Washington wanted his men to make their own shelters.

　C. It was close to Philadelphia so the soldiers could go buy boots.

　D. It kept the British, who were staying in Philadelphia for the winter, from advancing.

On the map above, find Valley Forge National Historical Park. Which state is it in?

_____

Name _____ **Date** _____

Activity 11

Sharks are a natural resource. Long ago, Japanese warriors wrapped sharkskin around the handles of their swords. Sharkskin is very rough, which kept the swords from slipping out of their hands. Other people used sharkskin, too. They used it before sandpaper was invented to smooth and polish wood.

Sharks are also a natural food resource. Shark meat is often eaten raw as well as cooked. Shark fins are made into soup. Long ago, there was no risk of sharks disappearing, but today there is a danger of this natural resource being used up. Today we have better fishing methods, bigger nets, and faster boats. Too many sharks and other fish can be caught, and this is a big problem. Some nets pull up every fish, large and small. Can one country say, "No more fishing!"?

Which is *not* a reason sharks are a resource that can be used up today?

A. There are more people needing to be fed.

B. Modern fishing methods catch more sharks.

C. Shark skin is easier to find in a store than sandpaper.

D. Sharks caught in one place can be frozen and sent quickly to another place.

Find Japan on the map.

Fish is an important food source in Japan. Why?

_____

_____

_____

Activity 12

A country has total control of ocean waters out to 12 miles (19 km) off its shore. It has control of fishing and drilling rights out to 200 miles (322 km) off of its shore.

Why would a country want drilling rights?

A. No one can fish where there is drilling.

B. Oil and other minerals are under the ocean.

C. People need to drill for water close to shore.

D. Most fish are caught in the open ocean.

Why might it be important for countries to sign treaties on fishing seasons and how much fish can be caught? _____

_____

Name _____ **Date** _____

Activity 13

Draw a cartoon about a resource. It can show why we need a resource, how to conserve the resource, or how or why we should recycle. It can be funny or serious.

Bibliography

Arlon, Penelope, et al. *How People Live.* DK Publishing Inc., 2003.

Associated Press, The. "First Grizzly-Polar Bear in Wild Confirmed." *Journal and Courier.* May 12, 2006: A3.

"Baseball," *The New Encyclopedia Britannica.* Encyclopedia Britannica, Inc., 1990, 1:932.

Biel, Timothy Levi. *Zoobooks: Skunks and Their Relatives.* Wildlife Education, Ltd., 1992.

Brust, Beth Wagner. *Zoobooks: Butterflies.* Wildlife Education, Ltd., 1990.

Ciment, James and Ronald LaFrance. *Scholastic Encyclopedia of the North American Indian.* Scholastic Inc., 1996.

Conant, Roger and Joseph T. Collins. *A Field Guide to Reptiles and Amphibians of Eastern and Central North America.* Houghton Mifflin Company, 1991.

Cunkle, Lorna. *Extreme Nature Knowledge Cards.* Pomegranate Communications Inc., 2006.

Davis, Kenneth C. *Don't Know Much about Planet Earth.* HarperCollins Publishers, 2001.

Davison, Archibald T. and Katherine K. Davis and Frederic W. Kempf. *Songs of Freedom.* Houghton Mifflin Company, 1942.

Foster, Ruth. *Nonfiction Reading Comprehension: Science, Grade 3.* Teacher Created Resources Inc., 2006.

————. *Nonfiction Reading Comprehension: Social Studies, Grade 4.* Teacher Created Resources Inc., 2006.

————. *Take Five Minutes: Fascinating Facts about Geography.* Teacher Created Materials Inc., 2003.

Ganeri, Anita. *The Story of Maps and Navigation.* Oxford University Press Inc., 1997.

Gifford, Clive. *The Concise Geography Encyclopedia.* Kingfisher Publications, 2005.

Glick, Julia. *"Texas Utility Tries to Lure Parakeets Away from Power Equipment."* Journal and Courier. May 5, 2006: A3.

Harris, Laurie, ed. *Biography for Beginners: World Explorers.* Favorable Impressions, 2003.

Bibliography *(cont.)*

Krull, Kathleen. *Gonna Sing My Head Off! American Folk Songs for Children.* Scholastic Inc., 1992.

Levey, Judith S. and Agnes Greenhall, eds. *The Concise Columbia Encyclopedia.* Avon Books, 1983.

McGeveran Jr., William A., Editorial Director. *The World Almanac and Book of Facts 2005.* World Almanac Education Group Inc., 2005.

Merriam Webster's Geographical Dictionary (3rd ed.). Merriam-Webster Inc., 1997.

Nelson, Melissa. "Ship Sunk to Create Artificial Reef." *Journal and Courier.* May 18, 2006: A8.

"Passenger Pigeon," *The New Encyclopedia Britannica.* Encyclopedia Britannica Inc., 1990, 9: 185.

Richmond, Todd. "Turbines in the Lakes? The Battle Is Brewing." *Journal and Courier.* June 7, 2006: A6.

Siegel, Alice and Margo McLoone. *The Blackbirch Kid's Almanac of Geography.* Blackbirch Press Inc., 2000.

Skoloff, Brian. "Florida Alligator Count High." *Journal and Courier.* May 29, 2006: A3.

Specter, Michael. "Planet Kirsan." *The New Yorker.* April 24, 2006: 112–122.

Sutcliffe, Andrea. *The New York Public Library Amazing World Geography.* John Wiley & Sons Inc., 2002.

Wexo, John Bonnett. *Zoobooks: Giraffes.* Wildlife Education Ltd., 1991.

Zoobooks: *Snakes.* Wildlife Education, Ltd., 1992.

Wulffson, Don L. *The Kid Who Invented the Trampoline: More Surprising Stories About Inventions.* Dutton Children's Books, 2001.

Zaunders, Bo. *Crocodiles, Camels, and Dugout Canoes: Eight Adventure Episodes.* Dutton Children's Books, 1998.

Zeman, Anne and Kate Kelly. *Everything You Need to Know About Geography Homework.* Scholastic Inc., 1997.

Answer Key

Standard 1

Page 9 Activity 1: C

Page 9 Activity 2: D; Maps can be used to show where countries, cities, roads, railroads, rivers, natural resources, etc. are located

Page 10 Activity 4: B; North; East; South; West; west; west

Page 11 Activity 5: NE; SW; SE; NW; NE; SW

Page 11 Activity 6: D1; E4; B5; B2; D3: C3

Page 12 Activity 7: Cartography is the making and study of maps; The equator is the horizontal line that divides Earth into the Northern and Southern Hemispheres

Page 13 Activity 9: latitude; parallels; equator

Page 15 Activity 12: United States—Northern and Western; Australia—Southern and Eastern; India—Northern and Eastern; Brazil—Southern, Western, and Northern

Page 15 Activity 13: Kingda Ka—Northern and Western; Top Thrill Dragster—Northern and Western; Superman—Northern and Western; Tower of Terror—Southern and Eastern; Steel Dragon—Northern and Eastern

Standard 2

Page 17 Activity 2: 1. yes 2. yes 3. country 4. no 5. east 6. yes 7. no 8. Louisiana 9. no 10. Alaska and Hawaii

Page 18 Activity 3: 1. Australia 2. South America 3. Africa 4. Asia 5. Antarctica 6. North America and Europe 7. Asia 8. North America 9. Asia 10. Australia

Page 20 Activity 7: B; A; An ocean is a large body of salt water that separates continents. There are four oceans.

Page 21 Activity 9: Atlantic; D; Indian; Arctic, Indian, Atlantic, Pacific

Page 21 Activity 10: Pacific; western; north

Page 22 Activity 12: Pacific

Page 23 Activity 13: Himalayas

Standard 3

Page 25 Activity 1: Superior; Michigan; Canada; Ohio, Pennsylvania, or New York; Chicago; Huron, Ontario, Michigan, Erie, Superior

Page 26 Activity 2: solar system; city

Page 27 Activity 4: B and C; B; A

Page 29 Activity 7: plane, boat, and truck; No because it was not as easy to transport goods; Labor costs might be less than the United States, the money saved in labor costs would pay for the moving or transport costs, or the items might be unique to that country.

Page 30 Activity 9: A2 or A3; B1 or B2; C1, C2, or C3

Page 31 Activity 11: C

Page 31 Activity 12: Jazz has ties to Europe because today the saxophone is used to play jazz music. Adolph Sax invented the saxophone, and he is from Belgium. Belgium is a country in Europe.

Standard 4

Page 34 Activity 1: A; Southern and Eastern

Page 34 Activity 2: Kauai is smaller than and northwest of Hilo; largest; 30

Page 35 Activity 3: B; B; False

Page 35 Activity 4: A; North America; Belize and El Salvador; Northern and Western Hemispheres

Page 36 Activity 5: possible answers—SW: Ecuador, Chili; SE: New Zealand, Papua New Guinea; NW: United States, El Salvador; NE: Japan, Malaysia; no

Page 36 Activity 6: housing, food, equipment; possible answers—Alabama, Georgia, Tennessee, Kentucky

Answer Key *(cont.)*

Page 37 Activity 7: B; Persian Gulf and Gulf of Oman; Gulf of Aden; Gulf of Mexico and Gulf of California; A gulf is a large area of sea that is partly surrounded by land.

Page 38 Activity 8: better soil and climate or cities with lots of work opportunities; Nigeria

Page 39 Activity 9: no; city

Page 39 Activity 10: A; NE

Page 40 Activity 11: C; west

Standard 5

Page 43 Activity 2: residential—retirement community; industrial—computer-parts factory; commercial—supermarket; recreational—baseball field

Page 44 Activity 3: B

Page 44 Activity 4: Carnivorous plants make most of their energy from sunlight like other plants; nitrogen; False; north—Virginia; south—Georgia; west—Tennessee

Page 45 Activity 5: India; Bangladesh

Page 45 Activity 6: B; The Arctic is a frozen ocean while Antarctica is a mass of frozen land.

Page 46 Activity 7: Northern Hemisphere; Southern Hemisphere; latitude; A

Page 46 Activity 8: Antarctica

Page 47 Activity 9: walrus, Polar Region; skunk, temperate zone; giraffe, tropics

Page 47 Activity 10: tropical; temperate; polar; deciduous; evergreen; coniferous; B

Page 48 Activity 11: B

Page 49 Activity 13: B; above; A

Standard 6

Page 52 Activity 3: An oasis is a watering hole with vegetation in the desert.

Page 53 Activity 5: C

Page 54 Activity 7: C; around 2,000 miles

Page 54 Activity 8: D; Rockies and Sierra and Nevada; Kansas and Nebraska; no bridges, oxen had to swim across pulling wagons

Page 55 Activity 10: B; Arizona, Colorado, Utah

Page 56 Activity 11: hard rock on the surface

Page 56 Activity 12: B; Mississippi River

Standard 7

Page 58 Activity 2: fishing; logging

Page 59 Activity 3: Earth's tilt on its axis as it orbits the sun. True; False; False; False; A; B; B; A

Page 59 Activity 4: D; B; A; B

Page 60 Activity 5: B; soil type, length of daylight, water, insects

Page 60 Activity 6: Kansas; Kansas; do not; do not; no; B—States north and south of one another are different distances from the equator, so they get more or less daylight hours and heat from the sun.

Page 61 Activity 7: yes; no; no

Page 61 Activity 8: D; the snow melts

Page 62 Activity 9: A; B; B

Page 62 Activity 10: D; A; All of Hawaii's landmass lies close to the ocean.

Page 63 Activity 12: B; B; B

Page 64 Activity 13: Atlantic Ocean; Northern and Eastern Hemispheres; Yes, because Camaroon is very close to the Equator.

Standard 8

Page 66 Activity 1: C; Venezuela

Page 66 Activity 2: C; yes

Page 67 Activity 3: D

Answer Key (cont.)

Page 67 Activity 4: D; A canopy is made of tree crowns. The crown is the top branch part of the tree.

Page 68 Activity 5: C

Page 68 Activity 6: D

Page 69 Activity 7: D

Page 70 Activity 9: C; Possible Answers: Bahamas, Cuba, Jamaica, Haiti; Dominican Republic, Puerto Rico, Guadalupe, Dominica

Page 70 Activity 10: False; False; True

Page 71 Activity 11: B

Page 71 Activity 12: Iowa; Mississippi River, Lake Superior and Lake Michigan;

Standard 9

Page 73 Activity 1: C

Page 74 Activity 3: Red Sea

Page 74 Activity 4: high

Page 77 Activity 7: A; A; B; B

Standard 10

Page 81 Activity 2: D; Arabian Sea; Indian Ocean

Page 82 Activity 4: D; Mediterranean Sea and Atlantic Ocean; NW

Page 83 Activity 5: C

Page 83 Activity 6: C; south

Page 84 Activity 7: C; Eastern Hemisphere

Page 84 Activity 8: D

Page 85 Activity 9: C; B

Page 85 Activity 10: A

Standard 11

Page 88 Activity 1: A; B

Page 88 Activity 2: D; no

Page 89 Activity 3: C; Bering Sea

Page 89 Activity 4: C; C; Canada

Page 90 Activity 5: A; B; A

Page 90 Activity 6: Baltic and North Seas

Page 91 Activity 7: A strait is a narrow body of water that connects two larger bodies of water.

Page 91 Activity 8: C; B

Page 92 Activity 9: An islet is a very small island; A port is harbor or a city with a harbor where ships can load and unload.

Page 93 Activity 11: B

Page 93 Activity 12: D; B; The International Date Line helps keep schedules straight for air flights and pick up and drop off of goods.

Standard 12

Page 95 Activity 2: Phoenix

Page 96 Activity 3: A; A; B; B

Page 96 Activity 4: none; Sears Tower; Monday; power from electricity or another source, such as natural gas, and building supplies; rural

Page 97 Activity 5: B; A; Caribbean Sea

Page 97 Activity 6: C; downtown—library and courthouse; industrial—wire and instrument factories

Page 98 Activity 7: C; B

Page 99 Activity 9: Appleville; Appleville; Appleville; Orangeville

Page 99 Activity 10: D; Asia and Europe

Page 100 Activity 11: Kenya, Tanzania, Uganda; Sudan, Uganda, Egypt; Cairo; A

Page 100 Activity 12: D; C

Answer Key *(cont.)*

Standard 13

Page 103 Activity 3: D; a curved area along a coast or shore where water juts into the land; no

Page 103 Activity 4: B; B

Page 104 Activity 5: north

Page 104 Activity 6: 1. lake = sea   2. water = earth 3. once = twice   4. impossible = possible

Page 106 Activity 9: D

Page 107 Activity 11: D

Page 108 Activity 13: C; A and C; Indian Ocean, Pakistan—Arabian Sea, Bangladesh—Bay of Bengal; India—Arabian Sea and Bay of Bengal

Standard 14

Page 110 Activity 1: lithosphere—mountain, canyon, sand, butte; atmosphere—dust in the air, air pollution, smoke, oxygen; biosphere—rain forest, insects, people, animals; hydrosphere—strait, sea, marsh, ice

Page 110 Activity 2: C

Page 111 Activity 3: D; *extinct* means no longer exist; Georgia

Page 111 Activity 4: 1,000,000; Tallahassee; C

Page 112 Activity 5: hydrosphere; atmosphere; biosphere; lithosphere

113 Activity 7: D; Formosa Strait; Tropic of Cancer

Page 113 Activity 8: A

Page 114 Activity 9: B; Mediterranean and Red Seas

Page 114 Activity 10: C; An isthmus is a narrow strip of land that is bordered on two sides by water and connects two larger land masses.

Page 115 Activity 11: C; Red Sea—east; Mediterranean Sea—north

Page 115 Activity 12: Terraces provide more surface area to grow crops; they also cut down on erosion as the terraces can be built up at the ends to prevent soil from washing off; rice, corn, wheat, potatoes

Page 116 Activity 13: D

Standard 15

Page 118 Activity 1: A; Lake Superior; Canada; north; Mississippi River

Page 118 Activity 2: B; north—Thailand; east—Vietnam; A

Page 119 Activity 4: B; A

Page 120 Activity 5: B; Brazil, Paraguay, Argentina, Chile, Peru

Page 121 Activity 7: A; Laos; Northern and Eastern Hemispheres

Page 121 Activity 8: B; Australia and Thailand, yes; Somalia, no.

Page 122 Activity 9: Sicily; D

Page 122 Activity 10: C; A treaty is an agreement between two nations having to do with peace, trade, or pollution.

Page 123 Activity 11: B; C

Page 124 Activity 13: D

Standard 16

Page 126 Activity 1: Renewable—oxygen, fish, plants, timber; Nonrenewable—copper, oil, coal, minerals; Flow—water, wind

Page 126 Activity 2: natural resources; Virginia, South Carolina, Tennessee, Georgia, Atlantic Ocean

Page 127 Activity 3: B and D; D

Page 127 Activity 4: no; Alaska

Page 128 Activity 5: yes

Answer Key (cont.)

Page 128 Activity 6: from United States: China—W, Australia—SW, Peru—S, Canada—N, Mexico—S; from Australia: China—N or NW, Peru—E, Canada—NE, United States—NE, Mexico—NE

Page 129 Activity 7: B; El Salvador does not touch the Atlantic Ocean.

Page 129 Activity 8: A; Guatemala—N; Honduras—E; Yes, because it is above the equator and below the Tropic of Cancer.

Page 130 Activity 9: D

Page 130 Activity 10: D; Iceland's capital is Reykjavik; Idaho's capital is Boise; Iceland

Page 131 Activity 11: Texas, Alaska, California, Louisiana

Standard 17

Page 133 Activity 1: Dwellings can be bigger today because we do not build them alone, we have bigger equipment, etc.; You would expect jobs to be different because many of us do not raise or grow our own food.

Page 134 Activity 3: D; B

Page 134 Activity 4: D; People come to work in the factories. They no longer have time to grow their own food or build their own houses. They have money they earn to spend on these things; Roads and more housing have to be built. This will greatly decrease the number of native plants and animals.

Page 135 Activity 6: A

Page 136 Activity 7: B; B; The prime meridian runs through England

Page 138 Activity 10: Atlantic Ocean; East Coast

Page 140 Activity 13: C

Standard 18

Page 142 Activity 2: Central African Republic and Benin; Africa; Australia and France; Australia and Europe; access to clean water, medical care, shelter, food, education, and jobs that are free from chemicals and physical harm

Page 143 Activity 3: B

Page 143 Activity 4: A; C

Page 144 Activity 5: B; Immunizations are one of the reasons life expectancy has gone up in many communities; Pacific Ocean; north

Page 144 Activity 6: B; United States; about 1,600 pounds(726 kg)

Page 145 Activity 8: A national park is a park owned and run by the federal government.

Page 146 Activity 10: D; Pennsylvania

Page 147 Activity 11: C; it is made of small islands, which means the ocean is fairly close to most people. (Almost 74 percent of Japan's land is rugged and mountainous, so most people live near the coasts.)

Page 147 Activity 12: B; If fish are caught before they can lay their eggs or when they are very small, the supply may run out.

Vocabulary Practice

Directions: Fill in the missing word. Each word in the list is used once. If you need help, go back to your Activities for this unit. Look for the words in **bold** print.

Standard 1: The World in Spatial Terms

Maps, Globes, and Finding Our Way Around

Eastern Hemisphere	grid	prime meridian
Northern Hemisphere	key	cardinal directions
Western Hemisphere	title	cartographer
Southern Hemisphere	legend	lines of longitude
cartography	symbols	intermediate directions
meridians	equator	lines of latitude
horizontal	vertical	parallels

1. A _____ makes maps.

2. The Hemisphere above the equator is the _____ .

3. The _____ of a map is a name that tells us what the map is showing.

4. Lines of latitude are also known as _____ .

5. West of the prime meridian is the _____ .

6. A legend is the same as a _____ .

7. Horizontal lines on the globe that run parallel to each other and never touch are known as _____ .

8. A _____ tells us what the symbols on a map mean.

9. The _____ is the line of longitude at 0° that divides Earth into east and west.

10. The hemisphere below the equator is the _____ .

11. _____ are shapes, lines, or little pictures on a map.

12. _____ lines go from side to side like the horizon.

13. Vertical lines on the globe that run north to south are called _____ .

14. The _____ are north, south, east, and west.

15. Lines of longitude are also known as _____ .

16. Vertical and horizontal lines are used to make a _____ , which can help us pinpoint places more easily.

17. _____ are the points on a compass, such as northeast or northwest, that are between the cardinal points.

18. East of the prime meridian is the _____ .

19. _____ is the making and study of maps.

20. _____ lines go up and down.

21. The _____ is an imaginary horizontal line that divides Earth in two.

Vocabulary Practice *(cont.)*

Directions: Fill in the missing word. Each word in the list is used once. If you need help, go back to your Activities for this unit. Look for the words in **bold** print.

Standards 2 and 3: The World in Spatial Terms

Mental Maps and Knowing Where We Are, and Directions and Where Things Are

transported	mountain range	ocean	mental map	isthmus	density
continents	peninsula	scale	mountain		

1. An _____ is a large body of salt water that separates continents.

2. A _____ is a map inside your head that gives you an idea of where something is and how to get to it.

3. A map _____ shows what a distance on the map measures in the real world.

4. A _____ is a group or chain of mountains.

5. A narrow strip of land that connects two larger bodies of land is an _____ .

6. _____ is how thick or crowded something is.

7. A _____ is a piece of land that juts into a body of water and is surrounded by water on three sides.

8. A _____ is a part of the land that rises abruptly and is at least 1,000 feet (305 m) above the surrounding land.

9. When something is _____ , it is moved or carried to another place.

10. There are seven large landmasses or _____ .

Standard 4: Places and Regions

Different Places, Different People

windward	leeward	population	gulf
vegetation	region	satellite pictures	reef

1. The _____ side of the mountain is the dry side of the mountain because the other side blocks the moist air.

2. A _____ is a geographical area.

3. A _____ is how many of one kind or thing is in one place.

4. A _____ is a large area of sea that is partly surrounded by land.

5. A _____ is a ridge of sand, coral, or bedrock under water but near the surface.

6. _____ are pictures taken from space.

7. The _____ side of the mountain is the side that warm, moist air (flowing up from coastal regions) hits first.

8. _____ is plant and tree growth.

Vocabulary Practice *(cont.)*

Directions: Fill in the missing word. Each word in the list is used once. If you need help, go back to your Activities for this unit. Look for the words in **bold** print.

Standard 5: Places and Regions

Places with Things in Common

residential	marsh	Polar Regions
industrial	tropics	Tropic of Cancer
commercial	tundra	deciduous
recreational	boreal	carnivorous
temperate	biome	Tropic of Capricorn
Arctic Circle	evergreens	Antarctic Circle
permafrost	coniferous	

1. A _____ area is where people go to have fun.

2. The _____ is a line of latitude in the Northern Hemisphere.

3. In tundra regions, the area underneath the ground that never thaws is called _____ .

4. A plant or animal that eats meat is _____ .

5. The Polar Region below the _____ and near the South Pole is called the Antarctic.

6. A _____ area is where people live.

7. The _____ is a line of latitude in the Southern Hemisphere.

8. A _____ is an area of wet, low-lying land.

9. An _____ area is where there are businesses and manufacturing.

10. _____ trees are cone-bearing trees.

11. Cool or _____ forests lie at the far end of the temperate zone in a few places and extend up to the Polar Regions.

12. The Polar Region above the _____ and near the North Pole is called the Arctic.

13. A _____ area is where things are sold.

14. _____ are trees that do not lose their leaves.

15. _____ biomes are areas without trees or forests that are found below the Polar Regions in the Arctic.

16. A _____ is a region with a particular mix of landforms, climate, animals, and plants.

17. _____ trees lose their leaves in the winter.

18. The coldest biomes are frozen deserts in the _____ .

19. _____ zones are the areas between the Arctic Circle and Tropic of Cancer and the Tropic of Capricorn and Antarctic Circle.

20. The _____ are warm regions that lie between the Tropics of Cancer and Capricorn.

Vocabulary Practice *(cont.)*

Directions: Fill in the missing word. Each word in the list is used once. If you need help, go back to your Activities for this unit. Look for the words in **bold** print.

Standard 6: Places and Regions

How We Think About Different Places and Where We Live

erosion	oasis	spring	mesa
point of view	butte	perspective	

1. A _____ is a hill or mountain with a flat top that has one or more steep or cliff-like sides.

2. _____ is the way things look from a given point.

3. A _____ is a place where water flows up from the ground.

4. When you look at something with a different perspective, you are looking at it from a different _____ .

5. _____ occurs when something is worn away by wind or water.

6. A _____ is a hill with a flat top that seems to rise abruptly from the surrounding area.

7. An _____ is a watering hole in the desert.

Standard 7: Physical Systems

Shaping Patterns on Earth's Surface

landform	pond	aquifer	hardiness zone	peak
prairie	glacier	plateau	volcanic vent	plain

1. A _____ is a treeless plain that is usually covered by tall grass.

2. A _____ is an opening in Earth's crust through which molten rock, gas, or air can pass through or escape.

3. _____ maps are made to show the average cold temperatures of different regions.

4. A _____ is a natural feature on Earth's surface.

5. A _____ is a small body of fresh water.

6. A _____ is a nearly flat region of land.

7. A _____ is a thick bed of ice that flows like a slow-moving river.

8. A _____ is the highest point of a mountain.

9. An _____ is a water-filled layer of rock, sand, or gravel under the ground.

10. A _____ is a large, mostly level area of land that stands higher than the surrounding area and is larger than a butte.

Vocabulary Practice *(cont.)*

Directions: Fill in the missing word. Each word in the list is used once. If you need help, go back to your Activities for this unit. Look for the words in **bold** print

Standard 8: Physical Systems

Where Animals and Plants Are Found

> food chain   extinct   ecosystem   food web   canopy

1. When something has died out and there are no more of its kind left, it is _____.

2. In an _____ , plants and animals are linked to each other and the land in a special way.

3. A tree _____ is made of tree crowns, or the top parts of trees.

4. A _____ shows how plants and animals are connected by what they eat.

5. A _____ shows how food chains are linked.

Standard 9: Human Systems

Where People Go

> dialect   immigrant   census   suburb   urban   rural

1. A _____ is a place where people live on the outskirts of a city or town.

2. A _____ is a form of a language.

3. An _____ area is a city or town.

4. A _____ is a count. In the United States, one is done every 10 years.

5. A _____ area is made of farmland or countryside.

6. An _____ is a person who moves to a new country to make a home.

Vocabulary Practice (cont.)

Directions: Fill in the missing word. Each word in the list is used once. If you need help, go back to your Activities for this unit. Look for the words in **bold** print.

Standards 10 and 11: Human Systems

People Patterns, and Buying and Selling Around the World

steppe	port	crafts	natural resource	exported
strait	sea	islet	culture	navigator

1. Our _____ makes us special. It is our language, religion, dress, and how we treat each other.

2. A _____ is a vast treeless plain found in southeastern Europe and Asia.

3. _____ are items, such as baskets or carved wooden spoons, which are made using a special skill or ability.

4. A _____ is a large body of salt water surrounded at least partly by, or next to, land.

5. A _____ is a narrow body of water that connects two larger bodies of water.

6. A _____ is a supply found in nature.

7. When something is _____ , it is sent from one country to another.

8. An _____ is a very small island.

9. A _____ is one who is skilled at finding one's way.

10. A _____ is a harbor or a city with a harbor where ships can load and unload.

Standards 12 and 13: Human Systems

Where People Settle, and How Earth Is Divided Up

currency	refugee	central business district	neighborhood	civil
national government	governor	delta	bay	tide

1. The _____ is often the main business area in the center of a city.

2. A _____ is an area of land shaped roughly like a triangle where a river deposits mud, sand, or pebbles as it enters the sea.

3. A _____ is a residential area with its own make-up (e.g., location, culture).

4. A _____ is a person who flees from his or her home for safety.

5. A _____ is a state's highest leader.

6. A _____ war is a fight inside one country between people of the same country.

7. A _____ is a curved area along a coast or shore where water juts into the land. It usually is smaller than a gulf.

8. _____ is money in common use.

9. A _____ is a change in the level of an ocean or a sea primarily due to the pull of gravity between Earth and the moon.

10. The _____ meets in Washington, DC.

Vocabulary Practice (cont.)

Directions: Fill in the missing word. Each word in the list is used once. If you need help, go back to your Activities for this unit. Look for the words in **bold** print.

Standard 14: Environment and Society

How People Shape Earth's Surface

hydrosphere	levee	biosphere	lock	reservoir
environment	atmosphere	lithosphere	terrace	

1. The _____ is made up of rock and land.

2. A _____ is a section of a canal that can be closed off by gates.

3. A _____ is a place where water is stored.

4. The _____ is made up of water.

5. A _____ is like a flat step or platform of earth cut or built into mountainsides.

6. The _____ is made up of living things.

7. Our _____ is made up of everything around us.

8. A _____ is a bank or wall built along a river to keep it from overflowing.

9. The _____ is made up of air.

Standard 15: Environment and Society

How Earth's Surface Shapes People

monsoon	treaty	hazard	traditional
adapt	salt pan		

1. A _____ is an agreement between two nations.

2. When you _____ , you change to fit.

3. _____ winds change directions twice a year.

4. A natural _____ is a danger like a tornado, earthquake, or flood.

5. A _____ is where salt has been left on the floor of a desert basin.

6. Something _____ is handed down. It is a way of doing something.

Vocabulary Practice *(cont.)*

Directions: Fill in the missing word. Each word in the list is used once. If you need help, go back to your Activities for this unit. Look for the words in **bold** print.

Standards 16, 17, and 18: Environment and Society and the Uses of Geography

Resources from Earth, Understanding the Past, and Using Geography Today to Plan for the Future

life expectancy	renewable	conserved	immunization
scurvy	flow	limited	

1. When something is _____ , it is kept safe from harm or being used up.

2. When a supply is _____ , there is only a set amount.

3. A _____ resource is one that we can grow or get more of.

4. A _____ resource is one in which we use the movement of a resource.

5. _____ is a disease due to the lack of Vitamin C.

6. How long one expects to live is one's _____ .

7. An _____ is a medicine that protects us from disease.

Vocabulary Practice Answer Key

Standard 1 page 156

1. cartographer 2. Northern Hemisphere 3. title 4. parallels 5. Western Hemisphere 6. key 7. lines of latitude 8. legend 9. prime meridian 10. Southern Hemisphere 11. symbols 12. horizontal 13. lines of longitude 14. cardinal directions 15. meridians 16. grid 17. intermediate directions 18. Eastern Hemisphere 19. cartography 20. vertical 21. equator

Standards 2 and 3 page 157

1. ocean 2. mental map 3. scale 4. mountain range 5. isthmus 6. density 7. peninsula 8. mountain 9. transported 10. continents

Standard 4 page 157

1. leeward 2. region 3. population 4. gulf 5. reef 6. satellite pictures 7. windward 8. vegetation

Standard 5 page 158

1. recreational 2. Tropic of Cancer 3. permafrost 4. carnivorous 5. Antarctic Circle 6. residential 7. Tropic of Capricorn 8. marsh 9. industrial 10. coniferous 11. boreal 12. Arctic Circle 13. commercial 14. evergreens 15. tundra 16. biome 17. deciduous 18. Polar Regions 19. temperate 20. tropics

Standard 6 page 159

1. mesa 2. perspective 3. spring 4. point of view 5. erosion 6. butte 7. oasis

Standard 7 page 159

1. prairie 2. volcanic vent 3. hardiness zone 4. landform 5. pond 6. plain 7. glacier 8. peak 9. aquifer 10. plateau

Standard 8 page 160

1. extinct 2. ecosystem 3. canopy 4. food chain 5. food web

Standard 9 page 160

1. suburb 2. dialect 3. urban 4. census 5. rural 6. immigrant

Standards 10 and 11 page 161

1. culture 2. steppe 3. crafts 4. sea 5. strait 6. natural resource 7. exported 8. islet 9. navigator 10. port

Standards 12 and 13 page 161

1. central business district 2. delta 3. neighborhood 4. refugee 5. governor 6. civil 7. bay 8. currency 9. tide 10. national government

Standard 14 page 162

1. lithosphere 2. lock 3. reservoir 4. hydrosphere 5. terrace 6. biosphere 7. environment 8. levee 9. atmosphere

Standard 15 page 162

1. treaty 2. adapt 3. monsoon 4. hazard 5. salt pan 6. traditional

Standards 16, 17, and 18 page 163

1. conserved 2. limited 3. renewable 4. flow 5. scurvy 6. life expectancy 7. immunization

Name _____ **Unit** _____

Geography Word Log

Word	Meaning
-------------------------------	---
-------------------------------	---
-------------------------------	---
-------------------------------	---
-------------------------------	---
-------------------------------	---
-------------------------------	---
-------------------------------	---
-------------------------------	---
-------------------------------	---

World Map

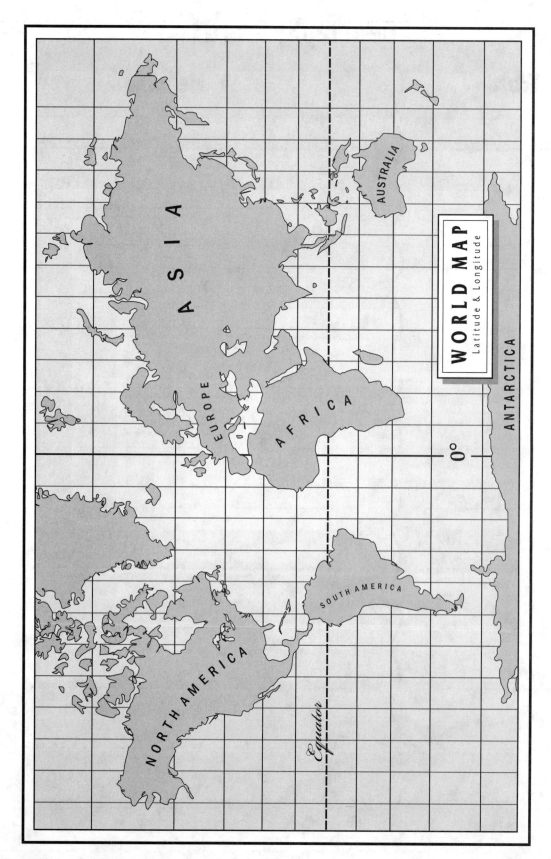

World Map

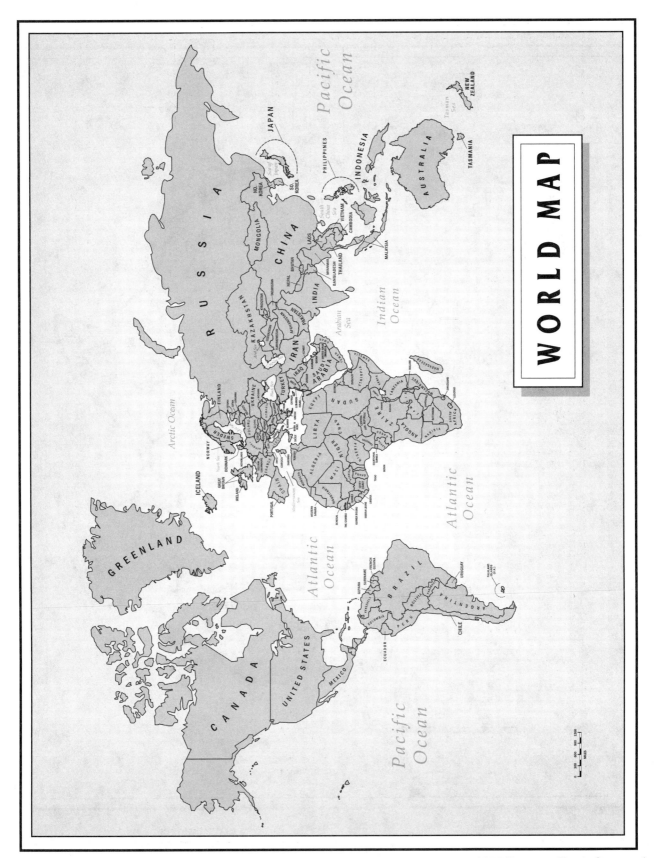

Continent Map: Africa

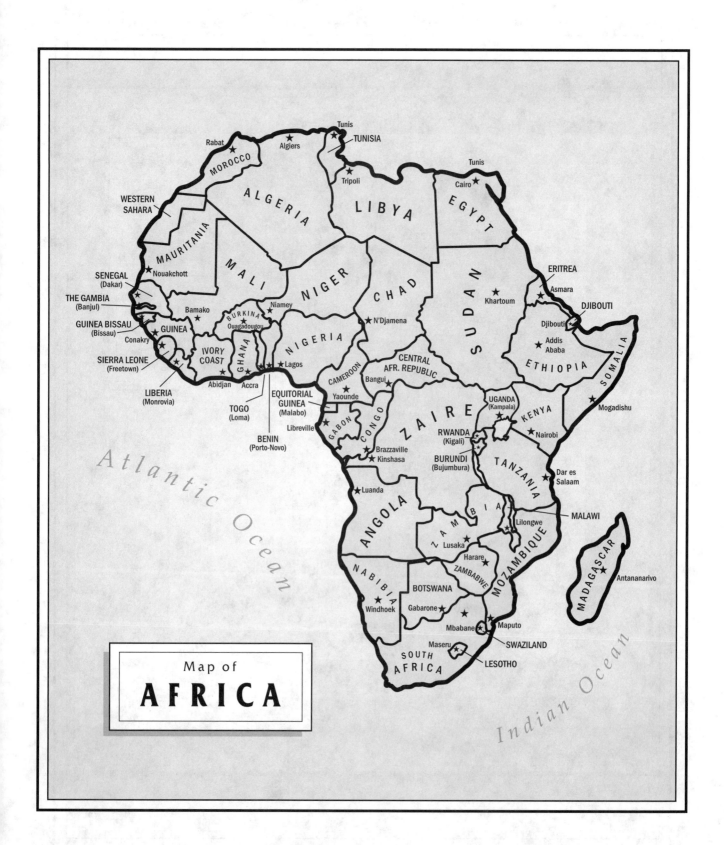

Map of
AFRICA

Continent Map: Antarctica

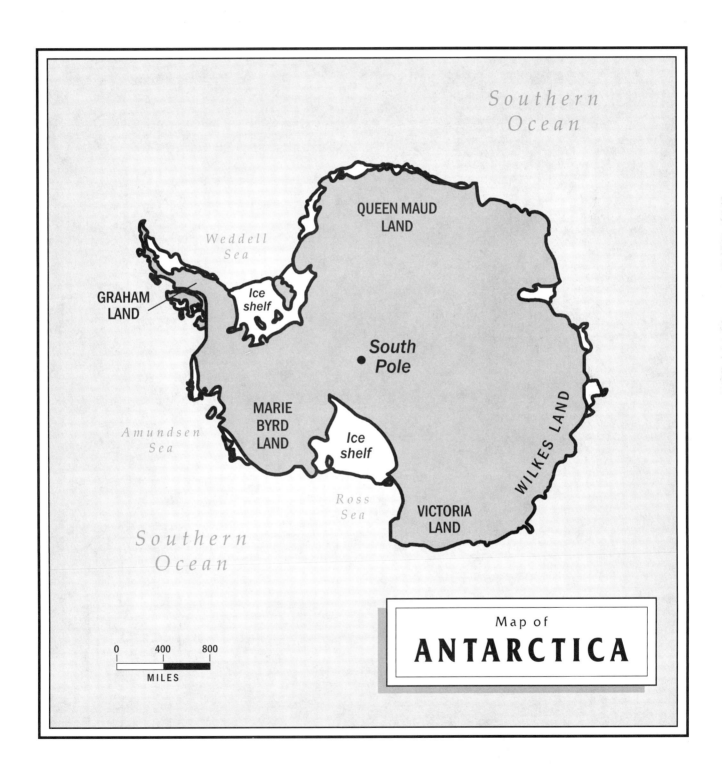

Southern Ocean

QUEEN MAUD LAND

Weddell Sea

GRAHAM LAND

Ice shelf

• South Pole

MARIE BYRD LAND

Ice shelf

Amundsen Sea

WILKES LAND

Ross Sea

VICTORIA LAND

Southern Ocean

0   400   800

MILES

Map of
ANTARCTICA

Continent Map: Asia

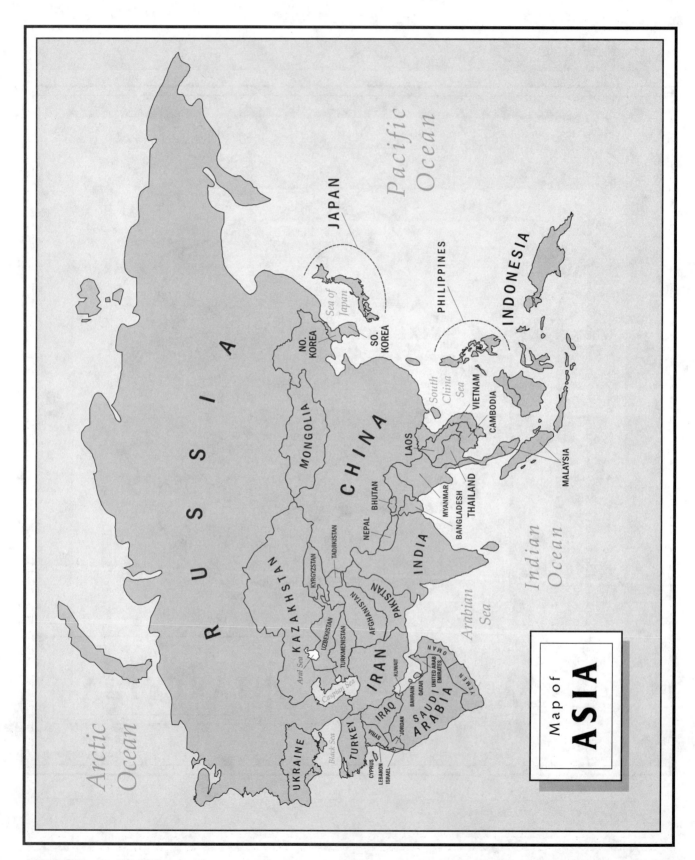

Continent Map: Australia

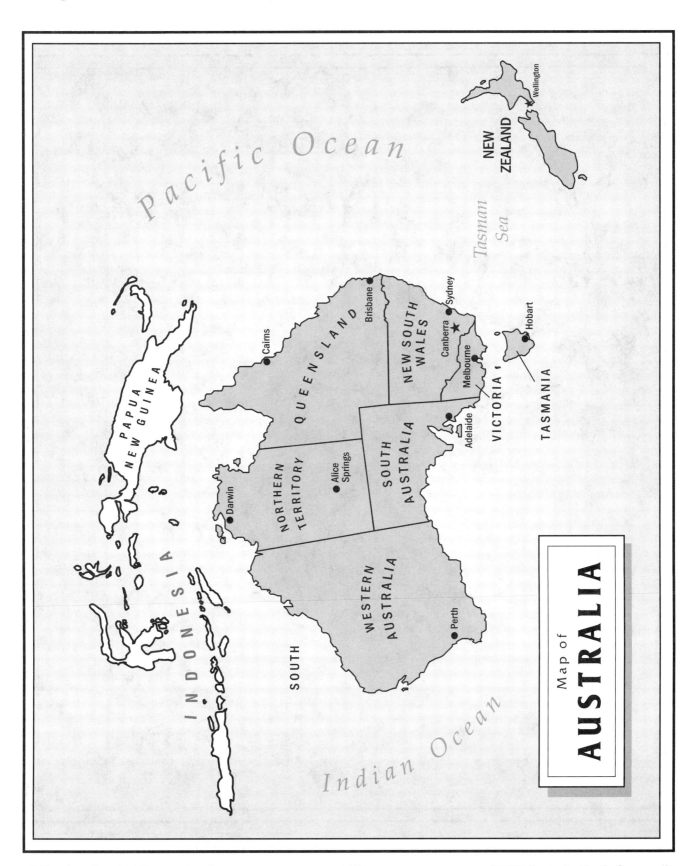

Continent Map: Europe

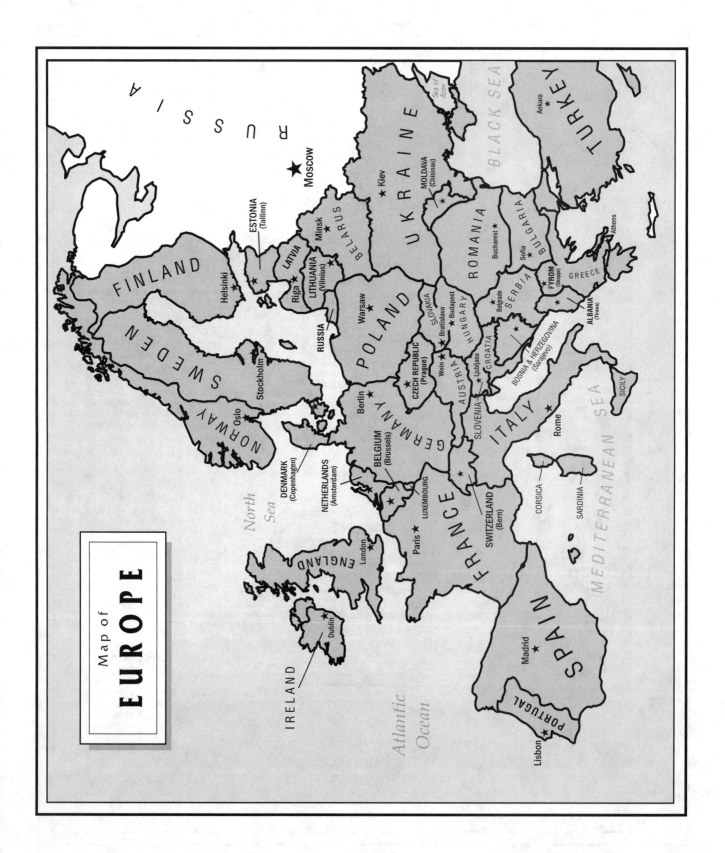

Continent Map: North America

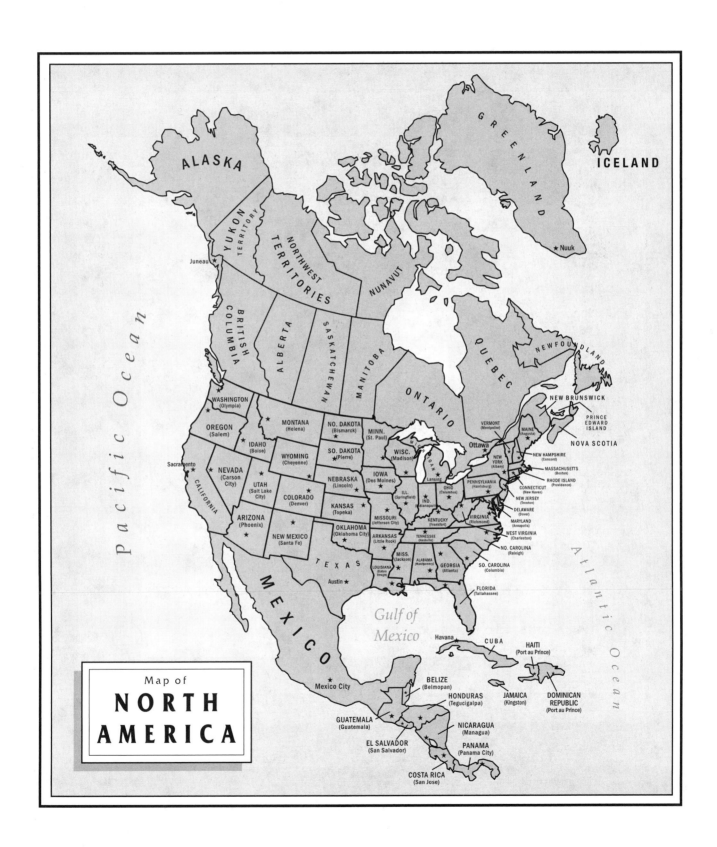

Map of
NORTH AMERICA

Continent Map: South America

U.S. Map

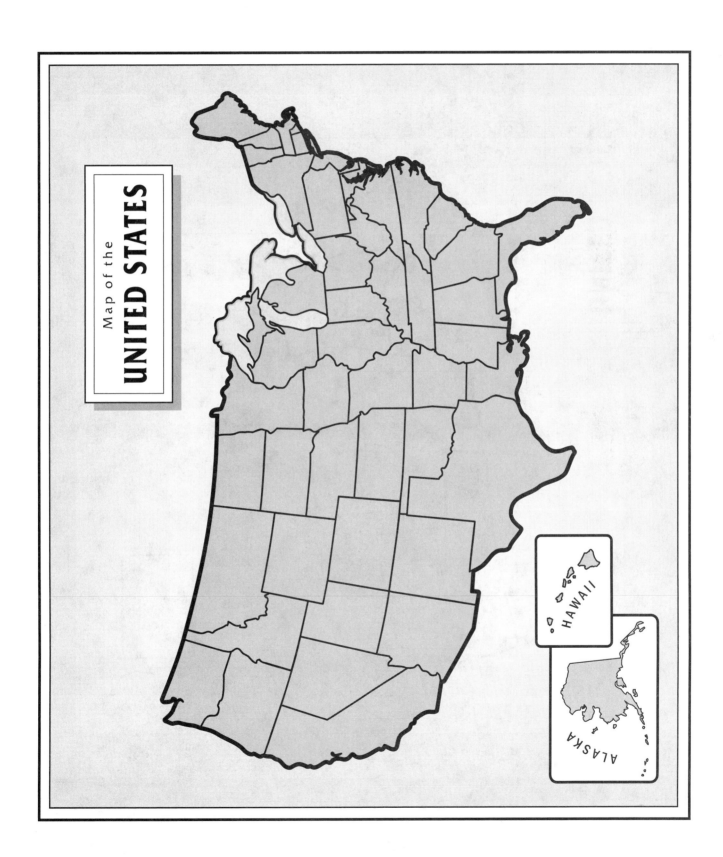

Map of the
UNITED STATES

HAWAII

ALASKA

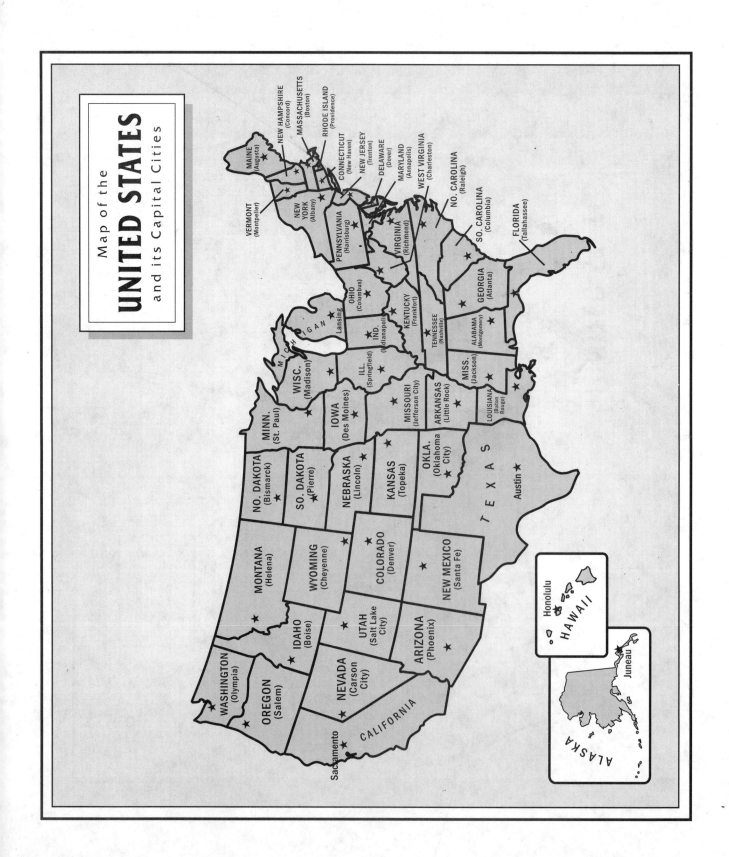

Map of the
UNITED STATES
and its Capital Cities

MAINE
(Augusta)

NEW HAMPSHIRE
(Concord)

MASSACHUSETTS
(Boston)

RHODE ISLAND
(Providence)

CONNECTICUT
(New Haven)

NEW JERSEY
(Trenton)

DELAWARE
(Dover)

MARYLAND
(Annapolis)

WEST VIRGINIA
(Charleston)

NO. CAROLINA
(Raleigh)

VERMONT
(Montpelier)

NEW YORK
(Albany)

PENNSYLVANIA
(Harrisburg)

VIRGINIA
(Richmond)

SO. CAROLINA
(Columbia)

FLORIDA
(Tallahassee)

OHIO
(Columbus)

KENTUCKY
(Frankfort)

GEORGIA
(Atlanta)

MICHIGAN

Lansing

IND.
(Indianapolis)

TENNESSEE
(Nashville)

ALABAMA
(Montgomery)

WISC.
(Madison)

ILL.
(Springfield)

MISS.
(Jackson)

IOWA
(Des Moines)

MISSOURI
(Jefferson City)

ARKANSAS
(Little Rock)

LOUISIANA
(Baton Rouge)

MINN.
(St. Paul)

NO. DAKOTA
(Bismarck)

SO. DAKOTA
(Pierre)

NEBRASKA
(Lincoln)

KANSAS
(Topeka)

OKLA.
(Oklahoma City)

TEXAS

Austin

MONTANA
(Helena)

WYOMING
(Cheyenne)

COLORADO
(Denver)

NEW MEXICO
(Santa Fe)

IDAHO
(Boise)

UTAH
(Salt Lake City)

ARIZONA
(Phoenix)

WASHINGTON
(Olympia)

OREGON
(Salem)

NEVADA
(Carson City)

CALIFORNIA

Sacramento

Honolulu

HAWAII

Juneau

ALASKA